THE GREATEST SUMMER

THE GREATEST SUMMER

The Remarkable Story of Jim Bouton's Comeback to Major League Baseball

Terry Pluto

PRENTICE-HALL, INC., Englewood Cliffs, N.J.

Excerpts from *Ball Four* by Jim Bouton,
published by World Publishing Co.: New York.
Used by permission of Harper & Row, Publishers, Inc.

Excerpts from SPORTS ILLUSTRATED ("A Magnificent Obsession" by
Frank Deford) used by permission. © 1978 Time Inc.

Excerpts from *New Times* ("Extra Innings" by Lawrence Wright)
reprinted by permission of The Sterling Lord Agency, Inc.
Copyright © 1978 by Lawrence Wright.

Prentice-Hall International, Inc., London
Prentice-Hall of Australia, Pty. Ltd., Sydney
Prentice-Hall of Canada, Ltd., Toronto
Prentice-Hall of India Private Ltd., New Delhi
Prentice-Hall of Japan, Inc., Tokyo
Prentice-Hall of Southeast Asia Pte. Ltd., Singapore
Whitehall Books Limited, Wellington, New Zealand
10 9 8 7 6 5 4 3 2 1

Library of Congress Cataloging in Publication Data

Pluto, Terry
    The greatest summer.

    1. Bouton, Jim. 2. Baseball players—United
States—Biography. I. Title.
GV865.B69P58   796.357'092'4 [B]   78-31646
ISBN 0-13-364927-X

For Bert and my parents

Contents

Preface

When I approached Jim Bouton with the idea of a book one hot, sunny day in the outfield of Savannah's Grayson Stadium, he was very quiet for one of the few times during his three-month stay in the Southern League.

"Look, Terry, I like you and consider you a good friend, but I just can't afford to be involved with a book right now," explained Bouton.

The Savannah Braves were taking batting practice and Bouton left my side to run under a fly ball.

Slowly, he came walking back, and then he picked his words carefully like a fussy customer sorting through oranges at a fruit stand.

"Everyone still thinks that I'm doing all this just to write a book. That's not the point of my coming back, and if word got out that I was cooperating in putting out a book, it would ruin my credibility."

I must have looked a bit hurt, because he added, "I'm really flattered that you'd want to do a book on me. It's a nice gesture."

"You don't really mean that," I said.

"Well, it is rather mercenary of you," he added with a smile. "But you understand my position. I don't want to be considered a gimmick."

Anyone who saw Bouton do his push-ups, run sprints, and train harder than his younger counterparts knew that he was no joke. Jim was as serious about playing ball as he had been twenty years ago with the New York Yankees.

So this book is not a Jim Bouton production; it is the result of research, interviews, and the observations I made while covering Bouton with the Savannah Braves.

He was friendly and helpful in our association as an athlete and a newspaper reporter.

I would like to thank those who helped, including Stu Livingstone, Roger Alexander, Dan Morogiello, Lelan Byrd, Bobby Dews, Johnny Sain, Dave Fendrick, Bill Veeck, Tim Graven, Jerry Royster, and especially Miles Wolff.

Others who lent moral support were my wife Bert, Ken Rappoport of the *Associated Press*, Susan Gorsky, and Bob Bevan. Once again, thank you all and anyone else I might have inadvertently omitted.

Part One
The Decision

1

Ride to Emerald City

Just a few hours ago, Jim Bouton was a Savannah Brave riding buses to places like Knoxville and Montgomery. He was a bush leaguer, another guy in Class AA.

The major leagues, which for so long had seemed light years away, stood at the end of the five-hour drive from Savannah to Atlanta. When he arrived at the Georgia capital, he'd be an Atlanta Brave, a member of the steak and jet set, a big leaguer again at 39.

This was the greatest night of Jim Bouton's life. He knew it and savored every moment like a connoisseur of fine wines. He rode along Interstate 16 alone, watching the white, broken highway lines.

In the past two years he had covered almost 50,000 miles. While he was just one of the players on a minor league bus, he had really made the trip by himself. Being alone was part of what Jim Bouton's minor league odyssey was about.

"When a man stands on the mound with a baseball in his hand, he is alone. He watches his destiny and holds his future in his hand. Nothing starts until he throws the ball and he thinks of nothing other than the next pitch and getting the next batter out," said Bouton, discussing the pitcher's role.

A man needs a goal, a purpose. This is especially true of someone at the crossroads of life, someone nearing 40. No one realized this more than Bouton.

On the surface, he appeared to have everything. He was a television star, a sports celebrity, and had what many considered an ideal marriage and a family straight out of a Norman Rockwell painting. There was plenty of money and an 18-room mansion in Englewood, New Jersey. The last fifteen years had seen him progress from a World Series hero to a best-selling author to a highly rated sportscaster to a situation comedy actor and screenplay writer. It had all happened so fast, so easily, almost like winning a lottery.

Jim Bouton had everything, everything but a reason to enter the second half of his life. He was bored with studios and scripts. Being a family man with three children approaching their teens wasn't easy. There was a need to leave it all behind for a time. He longed to latch on to something. Something different. Something which required total concentration and effort. Something that he loved and that would make him feel young again. He longed for something like baseball, where a man had a clearly defined goal—to get the next batter out.

So at 38, Jim Bouton, the celebrity, father, and author, rode away from it all. He drove to Knoxville, Tennessee, where he entered a period which in most athletes' careers would fall under the classification of "extra innings." In the dreary city of Knoxville, he became Jim Bouton the ball player. He had hopes that returning to the diamond might put everything else in perspective. Maybe in the simple game of baseball, answers to his other problems might surface.

As Bouton drove down the highway on this muggy September night, the problems of middle age still followed him. But being a big leaguer again made them more palatable. For Bouton, everything was easier to take when he was a major leaguer.

Alone in his 1976 Renault, loaded with luggage and health food cooking utensils, Bouton was more aware than ever that his fortieth birthday was just six months away. He turned on an all-night nostalgia station and sang along with all the hits of the '50s.

He was Jim Bouton driving into the past, entering a time warp. From the radio came the same songs that had set the beat for his first trip to the majors.

"I felt like I was driving to Emerald City," Bouton said of his trip.

Actually, he was like a middle-aged Judy Garland returning to Oz. The Wizard, Tin Man, Scarecrow, and Lion were gone, however.

He was the Rip Van Winkle of baseball, and on the ride to Atlanta, Bouton pondered what things would be like now. He also thought of the past, especially the last two summers. There were the gray days—being humiliated in Knoxville and Mexico and pitching with a bunch of castoffs in Portland.

Then he recalled the begging and pleading for another chance. Thinking of the sales pitch to the Braves' owner Ted Turner, which saved his tenuous career, brought back memories of those glorious months of winning and finding his youth in Richmond and Savannah. He thought of how the impossible dream burned inside him like an eternal flame while everyone tried to quench it.

On the seat next to him was a baseball. Bouton picked it up and instinctively held it by his fingertips in the grip of the knuckleball.

For two years, Bouton had hung by his fingertips, relying on the knuckleball to be a fountain of youth and a psychological savior. For Jim Bouton, the pitch was exactly that.

2

The Knuckleball

Jim Bouton and the knuckleball were made for each other. They're the perfect pair and the marriage is consummated every time Bouton takes the mound.

The knuckleball is a form of schizophrenia. It's thrown with the fingertips (not with the knuckles, as is commonly thought) on the seams; and the thumb, serving as a balancing board on the bottom of the ball, supplies its direction.

Other pitchers strive for speed. They want a strong rotation of the baseball on their curve balls and sliders, and control which will enable them to hit a catcher's mitt held at any spot behind the plate. The knuckleballer breaks all of these axioms.

First of all, the hurler doesn't want to overexert himself while throwing the knuckler; this causes the ball to spin and drift up to the plate like a batting practice offering. The knuckleball is thrown slowly, in a relaxed motion with a minimum of effort. On its path to the plate, it hovers like a planet out of its orbit. It has the potential to break in any direction. The pitcher, catcher, batter, and umpire have no idea where or if the knuckleball will move. Unlike a basketball player, who is sure his shot will go in at the point of release, all the knuckleball pitcher knows is whether or not his offering will spin. Then it is up to the air pressure, the wind, the time of day, and the gods to determine what will happen. One time it will hop up four or five inches, in another instance it might sink six inches, or it simply floats up to the batter like a big, fat softball thrown at a Sunday picnic.

Knuckleball pitchers have always been the sport's illegitimate children. Since their pitch is strange, the individual throwing it must be a deviant.

Hoyt Wilhelm, the best-known of the knuckleballers, pitched until he was 49. He was traded from team to team, not because he was an undesirable character or an unsuccessful pitcher, but because it was difficult for a team to find a catcher who could handle the pitch without spending most of the time chasing errant breaks back to the screen or suffering bodily harm thanks to its erratic movement.

Quick base runners love to steal when a knuckleball pitcher is working. A catcher has a rough enough time just knocking the ball down without worrying about catching it and tossing a runner out. A wild pitch or passed ball is always a real possibility.

When the knuckleball doesn't work, it can be hit for what seems like miles with little effort on the batter's part.

For these reasons, baseball is never quite sure how to use knuckleball pitchers. Wilhelm and most of the other knuckler pioneers were employed as relievers because the pitch hardly strains the arm and they could pitch almost every day. Wilhelm did make a few starts, and tossed a no-hitter in one of them, but baseball has always been at a loss when trying to find a permanent spot for the knuckleballer.

Baseball has also had a difficult time deciding how to treat Bouton. He plays the game on the field well or "as it's supposed to be played," as the managers like to characterize a hustling athlete. But in the clubhouse, Bouton is like the unpredictable knuckleball. His hustling and aggressive attitude isn't limited to just the field, and this created problems with some of his teammates.

From the start he always wanted to be a pitcher, on the mound, in charge.

There are a few kids in almost every neighborhood about whom people say, "they're naturals," the ones born to play, the names that will fill the sports pages. Usually, they are the pitchers and they bat cleanup.

Bouton wasn't one of these. He was a scrawny, unathletic child. He seldom left the bench and was known to his teammates as "Warmup Bouton." As a youngster, he would chastise the players behind him for their mistakes and generally had several characteristics commonly attributed to a spoiled brat.

Jim Bouton likes to say that he wins as many games with his stomach and heart as he does with his arm. "I can just will some things to happen."

It appears that Bouton simply "willed" himself into becoming a pitcher. At fifteen, he was cut from his high school baseball team, but he came right back the following season. He was already throwing the knuckleball, which he claims to have learned from the back of a cereal box at age twelve.

By his senior year in high school, he had developed into a better than average prep pitcher and the first of several self-promotions by Jim Bouton began.

His father had heard that Western Michigan had a nice campus and a solid baseball program. So he mailed that college some of the newspaper clippings of his son's better games with a note suggesting that Western give "this prospect" a scholarship. The note was signed "A Western Michigan Booster." Amazingly, Western Michigan fell for the ploy and Jim received some financial aid.

In college, Jim Bouton, "the world's youngest knuckleball pitcher," as he called himself, suddenly began to throw hard, faster than ever before. He was a "chucker." "A flame thrower." "A fireballer." "A prospect."

To this day, Jim has no idea where the blazing fast ball came from. All he knows is that he wanted to throw hard and he did. He willed it. He flung his body at home plate with such velocity and force that his hat flew off, a grunting noise came from his mouth, and it appeared as though his arm might one day just leave his body and accompany the baseball on its path to the plate.

"Warmup Bouton" suddenly became a star. Professional scouts watched his fast ball, scribbled in their notebooks, and stopped by after the games to get acquainted with this "hard-throwing youngster."

Big league teams were interested in Bouton, but not desperately. In the summer of 1958 he had gained some notoriety hurling in the top amateur league in Chicago. Philadelphia and Detroit offered him tryouts, but very small bonuses. Other scouts spoke to him, but had nothing concrete to say.

Once again Bouton and his father decided to market Jim's services. Using the same basic method that brought him to Western Michigan, they began writing letters. This is the note that was sent to about half of the teams in baseball by his father: "My son, Jim, is prepared to sign a professional contract by Thanksgiving. If you are interested, have your bid in by then."

The New York Yankees decided that they had better hurry and come up with an enticing offer. Bouton signed a contract calling for a $30,000 bonus from New York. The Yankees were the only club to respond to the letter.

As a professional, Jim just kept throwing his fast ball with the windup which knocked his hat off. He had minor league stops in Auburn, Kearney, Greensboro, and Amarillo.

Soon he was in New York. The kid all the "naturals" had laughed at was playing the Big Apple, winning 39 games in two summers, plus a couple of World Series contests, and becoming a household name like Mantle, Maris, and Ford.

He was the "Bulldog," a determined boy with short hair and the All-American style, playing to win. A real Yankee.

But in the New York clubhouse, it was a different story. The players told him not to talk to the press, or at least not any more than necessary. That wasn't Jim's style. He loved being a Yankee and all the publicity that accompanied that title. Seeing his name and picture in the papers and on television fed his fragile ego and helped repress the basic insecure thought that he might one day wake up as "Warmup Bouton" again and the major league dream would be over.

So Bouton talked and became one of the press's favorites. Hardly the polished media professional he is today, he was still far more articulate than the average athlete, and an attractive person to reporters. He signed autographs and had a tremendous rapport with the fans while the aloof Roger Marises shoved their way through crowds of admirers.

He pushed himself with the press and exerted himself in the Yankee clubhouse.

The team was holding an election for a Player's Representative who would deal with the Yankee management concerning players' complaints and problems. Traditionally, this position goes to a veteran player who is considered the team's leader. No one is nominated or campaigns for the job as if it were a political post. An election is called and the players just vote for the veteran.

Well, Bouton wanted the job. He approached it in the same manner he does everything: by being aggressive and outworking the opposition. He wrote a paper outlining his stands and ideas on what the players needed and could get from the management. His teammates saw this effort as "Bouton just acting strange again." He was trying to be the leader of the boys, one of the "naturals."

In the election he received only one vote. The "naturals" had repudiated him and he was treated as nothing more than "Warmup Bouton."

The 1964 season saw Jim revert to "Warmup Bouton" on the field, too. His hat still flew off, and his body slingshotted at the plate, but the arm was bad. The fast ball disappeared with the same suddenness with which it had arrived. His days as the toast of Times Square were over.

But Bouton was never the type just to quit. He's intelligent and he had learned a few things about pitching, enough to sneak by and remain employed. And every now and then he could fire the ball as in the old days. But those times came with the regularity of a compulsive bettor's picking a winner at the race track—just often enough to keep him at the seller's window with cash in hand.

Jim bounced from the Yankees to Class AAA teams in Syracuse and Seattle. By now, he was throwing the knuckleball once again, knowing the fast ball was a product of the past like yesterday's newspaper.

Finally, in 1969, he landed with the expansion Seattle Pilots of the American League. It was at this juncture that he took another gamble. It paid off in unimaginable dividends. Even a big dreamer like Bouton, who saw himself in the major leagues right up there with the "naturals" while everyone else called him "Warmup Bouton," never could have visualized this success. He started taking notes and talking into a tape recorder every night. Although he didn't realize it at the time, Jim Bouton was about to become the most famous .500 pitcher in the history of the sport. By describing his stints with the Pilots, and later the Houston Astros, he was to be hailed as the sport's poet laureate by his supporters, and a traitor by his critics.

He called the book *Ball Four*, and it killed his baseball career but opened doors to a new life. The book made millions for its publishers. Bouton hit the talk show circuit, visiting Dick Cavett, David Frost, and others who had never even heard of him before.

What made *Ball Four* more controversial than the slew of other baseball books was Bouton's honesty. Like a good gossip columnist, he dropped plenty of hints about the clandestine affairs of some unidentified stars.

"Ball players are not, by and large, the best dates; we prefer wham, bam, thank-you-ma'am affairs," Bouton wrote.

But even more interesting, the book had real people,

identified, engaging in activities not exactly appropriate for the legends of the summer game. He told of Boston star Carl Yastremzski not hustling, Yankee pitcher Whitey Ford cheating as he threw a mud ball, and Mickey Mantle doing quite a bit of drinking.

One of the most memorable scenes in the best seller was Jim's account of "beaver shooting" on the roof of the Shoreham Hotel in Washington, D.C.

"The Yankees would go up there in squads of 15 or so, often led by Mickey Mantle himself. You needed a lot of guys to do the spotting. Then someone would whistle from two or three wings away, 'Psst! Hey! Beaver shot, Section D. Five o'clock.' And there'd be a mad scramble of guys climbing over skylights, tripping over each other and trying not to fall off the roof. One of the first big thrills I had with the Yankees was joining about half the club on the roof of the Shoreham at two-thirty in the morning. I remember saying to myself, 'So this is the big leagues.' "

What also made the book a hit was Bouton's understanding of the sport and his feel for those who are a part of it. But baseball didn't remember this aspect. Bouton had "named names," and that was enough to ostracize him.

Baseball Commissioner Bowie Kuhn twice called him in for meetings to discuss the book and how he had betrayed "the best interests of the game" by telling the world that baseball players were really nothing more than little boys playing a child's sport with no parents to watch over them.

The New York media, which had always liked Bouton when he was with the Yankees, because of his openness and frank answers, embraced the new author by giving him maximum exposure. Between the interviews, autograph parties, and Rotary Club speeches, Bouton barely had time to suit up in the clubhouse.

Despite his claims to the contrary, the 1969 season was nothing special on the field for Jim and he was even worse the following year. By August of 1970, the era of Jim Bouton the pitcher was over. Now he was to become a star, a personality, a relatively wealthy entrepreneur by marketing himself as the main product.

Baseball may have been through with him, but he was a hot item in show business. Once again, he took the Big Apple. This time he did it on television every night at 6 and 11 o'clock on the news. He was Jim Bouton, sportscaster, seen by 11 million people every day in the capital of the media world.

The book enabled Jim to get his first television break, but it was his talent, intelligence, and hard-driving approach which kept him on top for five years, starting with WABC and moving to WCBS. The "Bulldog" had willed his way to the zenith again. He approached every show as though it were a ball game, and he usually outhustled his opponents.

Bouton may have been No. 1, but that's a position he never craved. He always enjoyed being the underdog. Then he could surprise them, outwork them, and get the public on his side.

This tendency, along with a flair for human interest in the news, was exhibited by Bouton the sportscaster. He spent one fall covering New York's Dickinson High School, which had lost every football game the year before. Another disastrous season was imminent for Dickinson. Bouton filmed every one of the team's games, their pep rallies, and their halftime pep talks. When they finally won a game, Bouton was there and the team voted him the game ball.

And there were more examples of his unique approach.

In order to gain a feel for his stories, he rode a bucking bronco when the rodeo was in town, fought a bull like a matador, and leaped off the roof of a speeding car through a ring of fire.

But contrary to what his critics claim, Jim Bouton is not a stunt man. First and foremost, he's a ball player. Every summer, Jim returned to the diamond like a devout Catholic attending Sunday mass. He pitched in a New Jersey semipro league, changing clothes in cars and once again being considered out of place by his teammates. Here was this television star in his middle thirties being a child, diving for ground balls and backing up bases with the ferocity and zeal of a college player looking for his first break.

"I played in a beer league on Saturdays after I quit. It was so informal, I would dress in the rear of my station wagon. I lost as many as I won, just having fun. There were 24-year-old guys with beer bellies hitting me and yelling, 'You're washed up, Bouton.' I was 35."

On the diamond more than anywhere else, Bouton was back in his element. Once again, he was the underdog. This time he was the old man trying to outhustle the kids, but in reality it was just "Warmup Bouton" taking on the "naturals."

More and more he felt comfortable on the diamond and less at home in three-piece suits talking into a microphone. He began thinking about a comeback, one of baseball's biggest outcasts making it all the way back. It would be difficult for him to find a greater challenge.

In the summer of 1975 Jim heard that a team in Canada's top baseball league was seeking a pitcher for the league's playoffs. Bouton contacted the club's owner, said that he wanted to pitch and was sure he could win. An invitation was extended and Bouton left on a baseball vacation to Calgary.

His trek to Canada convinced Jim to bring the glove and spikes out and start looking for a professional team who wanted a 36-year-old knuckleball pitcher. He won in Canada, why not in the U.S. minor leagues? Then maybe in the "Big Show," as Bouton terms the major leagues.

He took a leave of absence from television and pitched a few games with the Portland Mavericks, an independently run Class A team. More than 10,000 fans showed up for his first game. Bouton was back in baseball.

But this comeback was short-lived. Over the winter of 1975–76, ABC bought the television rights to *Ball Four* with plans to make the book into a situation comedy. Bouton had set up a deal whereby he would pitch for the Philadelphia Class AA team in Reading, but he postponed his baseball return and plunged himself into the TV project. He was a writer and star of the show. With the same vigor he brought to baseball and the news, Jim began the series. He worked eighteen-hour days and attended to almost every production detail.

The show was a dismal failure, cancelled after six episodes. The "Bulldog" had been beaten.

"I should have known things weren't going right from the beginning," recalls Bouton. "I showed up with two scripts and all these people were telling me that they were great. I had never written a TV script in my life until then.

"Basically, I still think it could be a success. A baseball team is like the army and there have been several successful shows with an army setting. All the people I was working with knew about was the laugh track and 'Gilligan's Island.' I was the only one who had any concept for the show, the only one who knew about baseball," added Bouton.

During his experience with the ill-fated *Ball Four* television series, Jim became convinced that he had to return to baseball.

"I used to sit in a room without windows writing scripts all day and night," recalled Bouton. "I felt this need to be outside. My body told me to do something physical. I have these voices in the back of my head and they told me to play ball. I listened to those voices."

Bouton's family reluctantly agreed to see him through his latest venture, even though they weren't happy about the idea of wandering through the minor leagues.

"Jim was almost exhausted by the time *Ball Four* was cancelled. He needed to play ball and we learned to understand that," said his wife Bobbie.

"Oh, my friends all thought I was crazy to be going back to baseball," said Bouton. "It was hard for a lot of people to understand, but easy for me. It was just something I had to do."

In the world of television, Bouton was a "natural." He had the wit, intelligence, and style of a star. Unlike his attributes on the pitcher's mound, these qualities were not something Jim had to work at and develop. They were a part of his makeup in the same way certain ball players can rap line drives in games without even taking batting practice. A close friend explained Bouton's situation in television to the *Atlanta Journal.*

"He was good on TV. It was easy for him. But like the old Peggy Lee song 'Is That All There Is?' when it came time to do things a second time and be innovative, he was bored. He'd lost his zest."

One thing which never tired Bouton was baseball. Now that he had put some distance between himself and the game, its attraction seemed even greater.

"I admit that I grow bored with a lot of things. But that never happened in baseball and that's part of the reason I came back," added Bouton.

There were other reasons for his return.

Simply put, Jim Bouton was getting older and didn't like it. He always exercised, watched his diet and weight, and was proud of his physique. He may not have appeared to be 39, but the signs were there. A wife, three children approaching their teenage years, and old friends with gray hair that could not be washed away in the sweat of daily workouts.

But that didn't discourage Bouton. He is a man of unshakable beliefs, according to friends. He is impossible to argue with once he's made up his mind. A brief conversation will reveal his self-confidence, his need to get attention, and his beliefs that he can accomplish almost anything.

Bouton could not have a bigger challenge, an area where he could prove his youth, than by returning to baseball. Here, the odds against success would be greater than the first time around. But this was a setting he liked. He could be "Warmup Bouton" in the world of the "naturals."

Also, there was the idea of conquering the knuckleball, a pitch only a handful of major leaguers had mastered. Baseball has little use for knuckleball pitchers and even less for jocks turned authors who changed the sport's image and got rich in the process.

This was the ideal quest for Bouton.

What if the venture failed? There was always television or another book. The money would be there. The worst that could happen was that Jim would be humiliated.

Part Two
Knoxville, Durango, and Other Places

3

The Search Begins

A few years ago it was not uncommon to hear of a man who was a financial success quitting his job, leaving his family, and doing something rash like joining a commune. These individuals often discussed their need to put things in perspective by looking at the world from a distance. They talked of "going back to the land," "working with their hands," and "finding themselves." Others, seeking their lost youth, took on a young lover instead.

Returning to professional baseball is the way Jim Bouton left the white-collar society behind and labored with his hands. The ball club was his commune, and toiling in small bush league towns like Savannah, Columbus, and Montgomery was certainly a change from the fast-paced existence of New York City. The game was his mistress.

But the quest wasn't going to be an easy one. In Jim's last major league season in 1970, he had a 4–6 mark and a 5.42

ERA. At 30, he was through, over the hill, washed up. That year concluded with his being shipped to Oklahoma City, where he started one game, allowed six runs in the first inning with his last pitch being clubbed for a homer.

"The knuckleball seemed to go home to wherever knuckleballs go home to," Bouton recalled in his book *I'm Glad You Didn't Take It Personally*. "Even Hoyt Wilhelm had that problem. Except his knuckler must have lived close by and took only short trips home. I think mine lived in Hong Kong."

In 1977 Jim seriously began the search for the knuckleball and himself. He hoped to find some answers in the game of his youth, the sport he loved.

Of course, this wasn't something he could explain to the owner of a baseball team. He'd had enough problems convincing the monarchs of the sport that he'd be able to make a comeback at age 38 despite not playing full time for seven years. Considering the ill feelings surrounding *Ball Four*, emotions still held by many in the baseball establishment, teams were not exactly opening their spring training camps to the knuckleballer.

Finally, Jim Bouton found a taker. He was Chicago White Sox owner Bill Veeck.

A baseball misfit like Bouton, Veeck enjoys sending shivers up and down the spine of the sport's hierarchy. He always viewed baseball as a game, and games are supposed to be fun. Therefore, Veeck did everything conceivable to have a good time with his team and the fans. Veeck, a man who lost one leg in World War II, has more health problems than a hospital waiting room full of patients. He never saw baseball as a life-and-death affair. He had fought his own battles to just remain alive and knew that the sport wasn't something of grave importance.

It was the winter of 1976 when Jim Bouton dialed Bill Veeck's number at Comiskey Park. Like anyone else who calls Veeck, Bouton was put directly through without having to battle a screening secretary.

"Bill, this is Jim Bouton."

"Yes, Jim. What's on your mind?" asked Bill.

"I want to play baseball again. You're my last shot because no one else will give me a tryout," pleaded Bouton. Bouton then explained how he had abandoned television and a large salary to pursue his dream. He told Veeck of his sincerity and dedication to this endeavor and how he was in the best shape of his life.

But the argument that most impressed Veeck was the fact that no other team would give Bouton an opportunity to play.

"Look, Jim, you know that I believe in giving everybody a chance if I can. So why don't you come to spring training," said Veeck.

When the press learned of Veeck's newest pitching prospect, they simply considered it another one of his stunts. After all, Bill was considered the Barnum and Bailey of baseball. He was the man who had sent a midget, Eddie Gaedel, up to bat when Veeck owned the hapless St. Louis Browns. He was also the first one to introduce exploding scoreboards, fireworks, circus acts, and other promotions to the sport.

But Bill Veeck was far more than a man who just liked a good practical joke. He really did hold to the philosophy of presenting anyone he could with a shot at playing. Under the Veeck regime in Cleveland, the first black player in the American League, Larry Doby, was introduced to a world full of skeptics. Veeck also imported the second black player in the American League, Satchel Paige. When Paige joined the Indians, he was 48 and a legend in the old Negro Leagues. Many thought Satchel was just another one of Veeck's fan-attracting stunts until Paige won five games and saved two in his first six weeks with the Tribe.

So Bill Veeck had gambled on ancient pitchers before and won. Maybe Bouton would work out. He had a knuckleball just like the White Sox's top hurler, Wilbur Wood. Also, Chicago was dead last in the 1976 American League standings, having won only 64 games and owning the worst ERA in the loop.

"We needed pitching and I figured anyone willing to sacrifice as much as Bouton had deserved a chance. At one time, he was a successful pitcher, so why not give him a shot? People would ask me if I was worried about him writing a book. I really couldn't care. I liked *Ball Four* and I've written a few books myself so it didn't matter to me," said Veeck.

Bouton was back. He reported to the White Sox spring training camp with the enthusiasm of a high school kid starting out on the professional baseball ladder for the first time.

Spring training is the best time in the life of a ball player. Jim Bouton is a perfect example. He came from the snowy north of New Jersey to Sarasota, Florida, where the Chicago White Sox hold their preseason drills. In Sarasota one doesn't need a jacket and the sun is bright and warm. The climate just seems to put everything into a positive light.

The pleasant weather is intoxicating. It induces lifetime .220 hitters to think in terms of a .300 season. Managers of perennial losing teams toy with the idea of winning a pennant and express this hope to the press. Sore-armed pitchers believe that their elbows won't feel as though they were being stuck with a needle every time they snap off a curve ball.

Optimism is contagious. Players willingly join in each other's fantasies about how this year will be so much better than all the rest. At least 30 percent of the ball players say they are starting over, beginning a new life. Such things as dissension and contract disputes are forgotten in the spring. All is good and right with the world.

It is ideal weather for dreamers, the perfect time of year for Jim Bouton.

Another nice thing about spring training is the fans. They are primarily retirees who sit in lawn chairs at the games. They really don't care if their team wins or loses and boo about as often as turtles fly. These people are purists. The game rather than the result is the important factor. They are like an artist who loves to paint but has no intention of selling the final product. The act is the essence, the source of enjoyment.

Spring training fans also have several advantages over their counterparts in the major league cities. At Allen Park, spring home of the White Sox, the fans are right on top of the athletes. It's a small facility (as are most of the stadiums in Florida) and the athletes mingle with the crowd. Since there is no pressure to win, players will act like human beings and make contact with the people. It is an excellent setting for all, and one that Bouton always enjoyed.

"Jim ran more sprints and worked harder than any player we had on the team," recalled Veeck. "At first we started him with the big team, but it was apparent that he wasn't ready for the majors right away. So we moved him down to our minor league camp, where he continued to work hard but wasn't that effective."

Nevertheless, the Chicago owner kept his promise and offered Jim a contract with his Class AA Knoxville team of the Southern League.

Knoxville is an old, dirty place in the middle of Tennessee's Appalachian Mountains. It's a town that came out of the Depression scarred and beaten. Bars line the streets because there isn't much to do in an environment like this other than drink enough so that one's vision is blurred.

The Knoxville Stadium is one of those 1930's Works Progress Authority (WPA) structures. It's surrounded on three sides by aging warehouses and on the fourth by a railroad terminal. Broken glass and litter abound like snow on a mountain peak. The color of the seats is army green with a dusty-dirty tinge.

Knoxville fans reflect the ball park and the minor league setting in general. For the most part, they are the people who toil in the warehouses and railroad yards. Their hands are calloused and hard. If you were to walk into any minor league park in the country, you'd find these people, the inhabitants of the "beer and a shot" class. They are a step above stock car and professional wrestling followers, but you're far more likely to find them in a bowling alley or pool hall than at a symphony.

Unlike the kind crowds of spring training, these blue-collar people are highly vocal, ready to rip the opposition and their team at the drop of a pop-up. Umpires receive the pent-up frustration caused by a hard day at work.

These people were as kind to Jim Bouton as possible, but he certainly wasn't a crowd favorite, and for one major reason. Jim's performance there was as bleak as the ball park. Putting it mildly, he was hit hard. Or as *Knoxville Journal* sportswriter Alec Simpson said, "Bouton was a great guy, but who needs a 38-year-old pitcher who can't keep the ball in the stadium."

In *Ball Four*, Bouton has a section in the back of the book titled "Tell Your Statistics to Shut Up." No matter how he tried to quiet them, Jim's numbers flashed a highly disturbing message. What else can be said of an 0–6 record and a 5.26 ERA with 11 homers allowed in just 53 innings.

"I had been away too long," said Bouton. "It just took me a while to simply get used to being back on the field. I had been away a long time."

Perhaps the best part of his Knoxville experience was the return to the game as a profession rather than as a weekend vocation. "I've always liked the idea of walking across a field with the organ playing and the dew on the grass," Bouton told a *New Times* reporter. "I remember thinking as a kid, wouldn't it be great to run out there and slide into second base! It's such a nice place to be. You can tell at once that it's set up for a game of some kind—the manicured grass, the nice white lines, the men in uniforms, the mound being built up—you know something important and exciting is going to happen there. They sure don't prepare offices like that for people to come to work in the next morning."

But a player has to do more than just savor being a part of a team. He must produce, and Bouton didn't with Knoxville.

"We tried to convince Jim in the spring that he would

have to give himself completely to the knuckleball. Wilbur Wood and Hoyt Wilhelm worked with him and told him to throw the knuckler all the time. He was reluctant to do that and seemed to think that he'd get his fast ball back," said Veeck.

Rather than just give up on Bouton, Veeck had his general manager arrange for him to pitch with Durango of the Mexican League. "Jim was just so sincere and working so hard that I wanted to do something for him," added Veeck.

The release shocked Bouton, however.

"It just seemed like Jim was making some progress when Knoxville cut him," said Bobbie Bouton. "Knoxville had the worst team in the league and their defense and bullpen weren't very good, so what happened was hardly all his fault. What really upset Jim was that he had an offer to pitch with Jersey City of the Eastern League just after he had committed himself to Knoxville, but Jersey City didn't want him after Knoxville."

The only place willing to open its arms to Bouton was Durango, Mexico.

Durango is a poor mining city, tucked away in the mountains 6,198 feet above sea level and fourteen hours from Mexico City and civilization. Hardly a Mexican resort, it will suffice to say that life there is difficult and poor. Its residents, almost all of whom toil in the unsafe mines, usually don't last until a ripe old age.

The only recreation in the area is the baseball team. In fact, baseball in Mexico is a thriving colt just beginning to feel its full capabilities. The fact that there is little else for the residents to do explains why most clubs in the Mexican League attract ten to fifteen thousand people each game.

Bus trips in this loop are notorious for their length and severity. The average trek is 14 hours, and with a few stops requires a 23-hour ride. The roads hardly resemble American interstates. They usually are narrow, dirt roads built for a man and his burro and not a busload of ball players. The food is hot, the water unsafe, and one could never be sure when a snake or scorpion would come crawling into the clubhouse.

The Mexican diet did not agree with Jim Bouton's system and he suffered from dysentery during most of his stay. The thin mountain air did little to aid the movement of his knuckleball, either, as his 1–4 record and 4.97 ERA attest.

One thing Bouton did find in Durango was anonymity. *Ball Four* had not been translated into Spanish so the controversy which usually surrounded its author did not follow Jim south of the border.

"Really, most people didn't know who I was. To them, I was just some gringo that had pitched in the World Series a long time ago," recalled Bouton.

It is said that an American player's surviving in Mexico is an accomplishment. If he manages to perform well despite such problems as the hot, steamy weather, the language barrier, hot food, and grueling travel, it is considered a phenomenon. Well, Bouton survived and at times showed some effectiveness, but not enough to impress the owners of the Durango club. After a month, he was released.

Once again, Jim Bouton was back on the telephone. He wasn't willing to admit defeat and accept the humiliation. After his debacle in Knoxville and Durango, baseball teams viewed him as a liability rather than a prospect. Who wanted a 38-year-old author-pitcher who couldn't get anyone out but could very well write an embarrassing book about your club? In the late summer of 1977 Bouton was a leper that no major league baseball club would touch. Essentially, he was through.

But there was one team that offered Bouton an open invitation to pitch any time the knuckleballer was moved to do so. That was the Portland Mavericks of the Northwest League.

In minor league circles, the Portland franchise was unique. All other clubs in the bushes operate under a working agreement with a major league team. The big league organization supplies all the players to its farm teams. It is also up to the major league club to determine which players are promoted, demoted, and released.

Portland was an independent, which meant that no major league club dictated its policy. Actor Bing Russell was the man who started the franchise in 1975 after Portland's Class AAA Pacific Coast League team had folded. It was Russell's intention to field the best team possible and be a big winner in the Class A Northwest League. Most outfits in this loop were composed of players right out of high school and college. These athletes were the ones with potential, people who would develop at some time in the future.

Well, Portland wasn't concerned about how an athlete would perform three years later. They just wanted the best players available who would do well regardless of their age or past. The team held open tryouts and signed several ball players who had professional experience at the Class AA level but were released because the major league club felt that they would never reach the big time. Russell gladly gave these players jobs, paying them $300–400 per month, and his veteran crew trounced the opposition.

The Portland fans came out in great numbers for this band of rejects. These players would remain with the team for the entire season. There was no major league club to take away Portland's stars under this system.

Another feature of the Mavericks was actor Kurt Russell (a star of Walt Disney movies and son of the team's owner Bing), who played the infield in between films.

In 1975, when Jim Bouton was first entertaining comeback notions, Portland invited him out to pitch a few games. The sportscaster did the news in New York during the week and flew to Portland to take the mound for the Mavericks on the weekend. On the night of his debut, Bouton drew over 10,000 fans and pitched his team to victory. By the end of the season, Jim had compiled a 4–1 mark and a 2.20 ERA. He was told to come back any time.

When the 1977 season had worn down and there was nowhere else to turn, Jim called Portland to see if they needed another Maverick. He was welcomed back.

At this point, almost everyone was convinced that Bouton had a book in the works. Why else would a 38-year-old seemingly sane man want to play with a bunch of bushers?

A search for lost youth was the obvious reason Jim was wandering through the minor leagues and playing next to guys half his age. This thesis gained even more validity when the knuckleballer changed his diet.

"The trainer in Portland kept talking to me about health foods. He told me that I'd feel so much better and be more energetic if I cut out all the junk food," recalled Bouton. So fruits, vegetables, fish, and chicken became his staples. He swore off sugar and red meat forever and influenced his family to follow this example.

Bouton stuck to his diet. He would carry a styrofoam cooler full of fruit juices and vegetables to every game. On road trips, a blender and other utensils for cooking such dishes as rice were part of his travel gear.

All of this made Bouton an interesting subject, and talk of a book followed him everywhere.

"Look, I'm not doing a book," explained Bouton to anyone who would listen. "If I was doing this for a book, it would cheapen the experience. If something went wrong, I could say that it would make a good chapter and that's not what I'm after. I'm playing ball because it's what I want to do."

This is the refrain Jim repeated throughout 1977–78. Most people didn't believe him, especially the guys who played behind him in Portland. They saw him compile a 5–1 record in 1977, but his ERA was an unimpressive 4.50.

Even though unsuccessful in 1977, Bouton remained a favorite with the media.

"Nobody took me seriously. I was like a guy in his backyard who was building a raft and planning to sail to Haiti. I was an interesting story and always good for some quotes on a slow news day, but no one thought I'd make it," said Bouton.

One newspaper took a unique approach to Jim's quest. "There was this guy in California who wrote a story saying that the only reason I was pitching was that I couldn't find another job," said Bouton. "It was strange; reporters would come around and ask what I planned to do if baseball didn't work out. I'd laugh to myself. Hell, I could easily take their jobs. I had been in the reporting business and was good at it. I couldn't believe that some of them were dumb enough to think I had nothing to fall back on."

But Bouton didn't want to go in front of the camera or become an author. "I still awoke each morning thinking I was on my way back to the major leagues," said Bouton.

Jim Bouton was on the comeback trail, but 1977 had served more as a detour than a road to the top.

4

The Perfect Match:
Ted Turner and Jim Bouton

While Jim Bouton refused to admit it, he was deeply hurt and embarrassed by his thrashing on the pitcher's mound in 1977. He knew it was going to be difficult and that a seven-year layoff meant that there was quite a bit of ground to be made up, but he never expected to be humiliated.

Most people thought that Jim would have been through with his baseball fling after the debacle of 1977. They felt that he was finished playing and the little boy would now go back to television and perhaps write a book about the experience. These were the people who obviously didn't know Jim Bouton very well.

All the difficulties, the trials, and the failures didn't tell Jim that he could not make it. It only said that the challenge was a demanding one, requiring more effort and concentration than he had ever put forth before.

And when Bouton looked back at the 1977 season, he had a good feeling about it. He was struggling, engaging in the toughest battle of his life and enjoying it. Physically, he was in better shape than ever, and his mental state was quite healthy even though his confidence had been roughed up by opposing hitters.

The knuckleballer was far from ready to abandon his dream. And despite the numerous setbacks, Bouton still clung to his dream.

With that goal in mind, he spent the off-season in a rigorous conditioning program designed to strengthen both his mental and physical tools. Each night he threw his knuckleball to a college catcher (who received five dollars an evening for his services), and Jim committed himself to perfecting the pitch. He was not yet ready to return to television and a normal existence.

Bouton spent his days searching for a team to issue him an invitation to spring training. He was well aware that this wasn't going to be an easy chore. Just what credentials did he really have to offer? He had won 39 games in 1963–64, but most of the batters he had mowed down in those years had retired. The country had seen five different presidents, another war in Asia, and a book full of social changes. Since then, as a pitcher he had been mediocre at best, and one can rely just so much on the past.

But Bouton was constantly on the phone, anyway. He knew that he had the bargaining position of a cow in a slaughterhouse. It was time for him to make concessions.

The Seattle Mariners, an expansion club which had a team ERA of 4.41 and a last place finish, was one of Bouton's early contacts. He offered to pay all his expenses and work out with the team's Class A pitchers. Seattle said no, adding, "If we give you a chance, we'd have to do it for everybody."

Most baseball executives, when they heard that Bouton was on the line, shuddered and ordered their secretaries to tell the former author that they weren't in, and even if they were, they wouldn't be interested in him.

At this point, baseball viewed Jim as an unwanted house guest who just refused to go home despite the fact that everyone had gone to bed long ago.

Discouraged but refusing to surrender, Bouton had seriously pondered purchasing a minor league team (with the help of his brother) just so he could pitch in the rotation. Another deal he lined up was to throw his knuckler in the Netherlands, a country where the grand old game was in the infant stage. There were also calls made to Japan and Latin America.

Jim had seen his pitching improve (although that was difficult for anyone else to notice, especially from a statistical viewpoint) and he believed that things would be much better a second time around.

Finally, Bouton got a break. Through a friend who happened to be the editor of a sailing magazine, he was placed in touch with Atlanta Braves owner Ted Turner.

The Braves were one of the teams Jim had telephoned for a job, but Atlanta General Manager Bill Lucas kindly informed him that the team was in the middle of a youth movement and they had no room for a middle-aged hurler. Bouton, however, had never spoken with Turner.

Many say that Turner and Jim were a perfect match of personalities. Both had large egos, tended to be brash and flamboyant, and were considered mavericks in the sport. Baseball Commissioner Bowie Kuhn, who had censured Bouton over *Ball Four*, had also suspended Turner when the Atlanta owner lured San Francisco outfielder Gary Matthews away from the Giants. These two men had many similarities (including their age), but the thing they shared most were enemies.

If there was anyone in baseball viewed as more of a rebel than Jim Bouton, it was Ted Turner. The son of a Georgia advertising man, Ted took control of the family business after his father committed suicide leaving an incredible total of $6 million in debts.

Turner has a vivid memory of his father's final days, and that had a great bearing on the type of individual Ted became. "My father was working too hard, drinking too much, popping pills, and he was sick all the time. The pressure finally got to him. He put a bullet through his head with the same gun he taught me to shoot with. At the end, the banks wouldn't even honor the checks for his funeral," Turner told *Sports Illustrated.*

So it was up to young Ted—a free spirit until then, who publicly admits to being thrown out of a few high schools and college—to save the business. Turner not only reestablished the family's reputation, he became a legend.

His father had made money in outdoor signs. Ted expanded into all facets of the advertising industry, including television. He is the owner of WTCG TV-17, a cable station which is seen in 36 states and part of Canada. The station is very prosperous, relying on a diet of movies, sports (including the Atlanta Braves), and old situation comedy reruns like "Hogan's Heroes" and "I Love Lucy" to attract an audience. Many say that Turner has the closest thing America has to a fourth television network.

Eventually, Turner grew tired of paying huge sums of money to secure the television rights to Atlanta Braves baseball. The team was struggling on the field and its books were a collage of red ink. Rumors abounded about the team moving to other cities such as New Orleans. Ted wanted to keep the Braves in Atlanta and on his TV screen, so he bought the club despite having only a rudimentary knowledge of the sport. He had never heard of the infield fly rule and called the umpires, "referees."

Actually, Turner's sport was sailing, which he had learned while growing up in Savannah. Going out in the boat was not something Ted just did on Sunday afternoons as some men play golf; he was an excellent sailor, one of the best in the world and a winner of the America's Cup, yachting's ultimate award.

As a baseball team owner, Turner tried to sell his product like a new kind of cereal. There were enough commercials to numb the average viewer, and promotions were the norm. Ostrich races, high wire acts, fireworks, and many other imaginative stunts were part of Turner's baseball style. One who enjoyed mingling, Turner wasn't afraid to spend time in the dressing room and play poker with his players. Ted joined right in with the extra fun and games. His most noted trick was winning a race by pushing a baseball from home plate to first base with his nose.

"Ted Turner is every kid who ever got loose in Disney World," is the way Philadelphia 76ers General Manager Pat Williams characterized him.

Obviously, Ted was not the conservative, dignified, and benevolent type of baseball executive who ran most of the teams. If he were, Bouton would never have had a chance.

One day over the winter Jim Bouton and Ted Turner met and took an instant liking to each other. Jim had spoken to other owners about voices in the back of his head and "willing" things to happen and received the same look that a disciple of Karl Marx would get at a John Birch Society meeting. Ted once said, "I have a seemingly endless supply of bull," and he respects a man who has the same quality. As Jim talked and talked and talked, Turner was impressed.

"He sounded like he could deliver on what he said. I like people who do what they say they can," said Turner. Being an athlete, the millionaire saw nothing unusual about Bouton's wanting to pitch when the calendar said sit. "Hell, who could blame him for wanting to play. Ask Johnny Sain and Warren Spahn if they'd like to pitch again. You don't get old when you play baseball. You stay involved in the game and you stay young. You don't get old when you play games. When you grow up, you grow old and your dreams die. I never want to stop dreaming," explained Turner.

It was quite clear that Bouton's vision, as much as anything else, convinced Turner. Not having a baseball background, things like statistics and age didn't bother him. Jim's quest caught the interest of Turner. So now Bouton had found a team ready to give him a chance.

Explaining his decision, Turner said, "I already have one 39-year-old knuckleballer (Phil Niekro) and he's my best pitcher. With our pitching, we have to look at a lot of people. Besides, Bouton is entertaining to have around."

Bouton knew that this was probably his last chance. Atlanta probably had the worst pitching staff in baseball. They had finished dead last in 1977. If they didn't want him, who would? Another factor which added to the importance of this opportunity was that Jim's money was beginning to run out. He had cashed in the college savings of his three children, sold his summer house on a lake, and moved from a $125,000 home to a comfortable one worth $75,000.

Since the television series had been cancelled, he had brought in little cash, his average minor league income being about $1,000 per month during the season. Unlike other athletes who have nothing but their physical ability to bring in a paycheck, Bouton could always return to television and a handsome salary if necessary. But that possibility did nothing to alleviate his family's immediate problems.

When February came, Bouton left for Orlando, Florida, and Rollins College, where he had arranged to work out with that school's baseball team. It was essential for him to be in peak physical condition from the start of spring training, since he would receive few opportunities. Jim Bouton was back on the comeback trail and he was traveling alone. His family remained in the Englewood area and hoped for the best.

The Atlanta Braves train in West Palm Beach, Florida, an aging resort town which had been in the middle of its peak years when Jim Bouton was born. West Palm is the minor leagues compared to the large nearby tourist havens of Fort Lauderdale and Miami, but Bouton was happy just to be there, even if he was a second-class citizen in camp. He worked with the Class AA pitchers, young guys who had just started shaving and remembered seeing that old knuckle-baller in a Yankee uniform on their baseball cards.

Basically Jim toiled in anonymity. He received little attention from the media, and the few articles about him were skeptical of his motives and sincerity. But some of the Braves' minor league coaches watched the pitcher.

"Bouton was always doing more sprints and exercises than anyone else," said Tommie Aaron, manager of Atlanta's Class AAA Richmond club and brother of all-time home run king and Braves Minor League Director Hank Aaron.

The young players also noticed. "Jim was probably the hardest worker in camp. That impressed a lot of the players, but most of the guys didn't know what he was up to," said Stu Livingstone, who later became Bouton's roommate with the Savannah Braves.

During the spring, Bouton was treated as an outcast. Everyone acted as though he didn't belong.

"The players were very leery of him," said Livingstone. "Everybody thought he was weird and working on another book. Nobody wanted to be in it.

"I had read *Ball Four* a couple of times and liked it. One day I went out to get a pizza with him just to see what kind of a guy he was. I was like everybody else, I was very cautious around him," added Stu.

It was quite obvious that the only man who wanted Jim Bouton in camp was owner Ted Turner. In an attempt to keep the boss happy, the Braves' brass let Jim pitch in a few minor league exhibition contests. But these games were avoided by the team's decision makers.

"No one really saw me pitch," said Bouton. "And that's why they were surprised to find out that I had a great spring. I gave up only two runs in twelve innings."

Perhaps Bouton's success was news to the Atlanta front office, but their minds had already been made up about the knuckleballer before the first pitch of the spring. It was the final day of camp and Jim had just finished running his sprints when Braves Minor League Pitching Coach Ken Rowe called to him.

"Hank Aaron wants to see you in his office," said Rowe.

"What about?" asked Bouton.

"Just go see Hank," replied Rowe.

Bouton knew the message Aaron would deliver. When a bush leaguer is summoned to the Minor League Director's office, odds were that a ticket home was awaiting him. That's the way baseball operates.

Aaron came right to the point after Jim arrived.

"You're released," said Aaron.

"Why?" asked Bouton.

"You're too old," said Aaron.

"Why didn't you tell me that March first. I'm as old now as I was at the start of spring training."

"Well, Ted wanted you to have a chance," said Aaron.

"Okay, Hank, just don't announce it yet and don't clean out my locker. I'm going out to the field and work out," said Bouton. He did a few push-ups before heading into the clubhouse to change.

Jim tried to give the other players the impression that he was just leaving for a doctor's appointment. In reality, he caught the next plane out of West Palm to Atlanta. Bouton didn't want his teammates and the press to know he had been cut, in order to protect Aaron should Turner overrule his farm director.

"Everybody knew what happened when Jim went to Aaron's office," said Livingstone. "It spread all over camp. You can't keep it quiet when a guy gets cut. I was sorry to hear that he got the ax because he had had a good spring, but I thought that the Braves cut a lot of guys even more deserving than Bouton."

Six hours after being informed that he was finished, Jim Bouton stood in Ted Turner's Atlanta office.

"I had the best spring of anyone there," Bouton told Turner, "but I'm not here to talk statistics. I'm here to sell myself as a person. I've been a successful ball player, author, and television reporter and actor. And I work harder than anyone else you have."

Turner listened respectfully, in awe of what he instantly recognized as a super sales pitch.

"I'm a winner just like you," said Bouton. "I'm a maverick in the same way you are and you made it big. You won the America's Cup."

Bouton brought out a few more similarities between himself as a ball player and Ted Turner as a sailor. After ten minutes, Turner asked the pitcher a rhetorical question.

"Why does an intelligent guy like you want to play baseball? Hell, I know why," said Turner, picking up the telephone.

The man at the other end of Ted's line was Bill Lucas.

"We've got to find a place for Bouton. He's no dummy," said Turner.

"What should we do with him?" asked Lucas.

"I don't know, why don't we let him pitch batting practice in Richmond," said Turner, following up on a suggestion Bouton had made earlier to him.

It was Jim Bouton's mouth even more than his arm which kept his comeback alive. But in Richmond, the Braves Class AAA team, Jim would have to do some talking with his knuckleball if he hoped to stay around much longer.

5

"I'm a Choreographer"

Arriving in Richmond, Jim Bouton was feeling very good about himself. He had done what few pro athletes can claim: he talked his way out of a release. In almost any business, the pink slip is the final chapter, the end. But Bouton was writing an epilogue which would soon grow into an unbelievable tale of its own.

"I am not only a pitcher, I'm a choreographer," is the way Bouton talked of the events surrounding his comeback. He was dreaming things, making plans, and they were happening.

But there was more than Jim's choreography at work here. He was on a lucky streak.

There was no way Bouton could have made it back to professional baseball after the disaster with the White Sox organization the previous year had there not been an owner like Ted Turner. Turner has been classified by some as eccentric himself, and he appreciated the world of Jim Bouton. There was no way Bouton could have planned that Turner would own one of the worst teams in professional baseball and be in desperate need of pitching help. And there was no way short of pure blind luck that in Richmond Jim Bouton could have been reunited with the man who had influenced his pitching more than any other individual.

Coaching in Richmond after decades of being a big league pitching tutor was Johnny Sain. For a month Sain would be working daily with one of his prize pupils of almost twenty years before.

Somehow, he did not look quite right in civilian clothes. There was something wrong with the mod style he was wearing. He came into the Richmond clubhouse, quickly shed these clothes and started to put on his uniform. For most men over 35, particularly with the new double knits, a baseball uniform is unflattering. The jersey is too tight, it shows the bulges, and any middle-aged man running around in knickers is incongruous. But this 59-year-old man, tall with white stringy hair and deep-set eyes, did not look bad in a baseball uniform.

As he slowly put it on, one realized that this was more than a simple act of dressing, it was close to a ritual. He was casual with his street clothes, but there was nothing nonchalant in the way he put on his uniform. He dressed carefully, making certain the socks and sanitary hose underneath were folded correctly, and he repeated the process several times until he had done it to the specifications he felt were proper.

The man was Johnny Sain. He has been pulling on uniforms since 1936, when he pitched for someplace known as Osceola in the Northeast Arkansas League, a Class D circuit, long since abandoned. In some quarters he is the most respected pitching coach in the game. Detroit, Minnesota, and the Yankees all made the World Series while he was instructing their hurlers. Now he was in the minors. He had a big league offer to coach in Oakland for the 1978 season, but

Ted Turner held him to a contract and sent him to Richmond.

Jim Bouton has a reverential view of Johnny Sain. In *Ball Four* he said, "Sain is not only the greatest pitching coach who ever lived, he's a man who tells the truth." Eight years later, Bouton still felt the same way.

Sain is a quiet, almost shy man, and he does not talk easily unless the subject is pitching. Then he can go on forever. It has been said that Johnny is one-dimensional, that all he knows is pitching, but the dimensions of Sain's pitching are multifaceted. He thinks of himself primarily as a tutor, and he says, "The secret of teaching is to repeat yourself without being boring."

When he was asked about Bouton, he smiled and started talking, but he is not a man to come directly to the point. His opening statement was, "I don't give up on anyone until they give up on themselves." He discussed all the other 39-year-old pitchers who were successful, naming Warren Spahn, Don McMahon, and a few others. He noted their success without really touching on Bouton.

Another question was asked. How did he view Bouton when, as a batting practice pitcher for Richmond, he asked for help? Sain smiled again. "I loved it."

Wasn't his job with Richmond to aid the young pitchers on the staff? Sain shook his head. "I'll spend my time with the tenth man on the staff if he's the one asking for help." He looked out to the clubhouse where the Richmond team was dressing. "Some of those pitchers don't want my help, and so I can't give it. I can only help those who ask for it."

He then recalled the Jim Bouton he knew seventeen years before. "You know, he has the same enthusiasm as when he was a rookie in New York."

Back then Bouton was just one of many pitchers in the Yankee camp, destined to report to their Texas League farm club. But one day after a workout he came up and begged for help from Johnny Sain. Sain liked that.

Even then Bouton had a knuckleball, and he questioned the Yankee pitching coach about it, asking if he should work on it more. Sain asked him what his best pitch was. When Bouton said it was a fast ball, he told the rookie to concentrate on that weapon. And Sain remembered the exact percentages, the total time, he told Bouton to spend on each of his pitches. Bouton followed the advice. Johnny does not forget much, particularly his former pupils.

Sain continued talking, some about Bouton, but mostly about pitching, and even though the team was out at batting practice and he should have been working with his pitchers, he still rambled on about the aspect of the sport he knows best.

As with most dedicated people, people who are in love with their work, there is a spark to this man who has spent his life trying to discover different ways to throw a ball. He does not even care that much about other areas of the game. On the two occasions when Richmond Manager Tommie Aaron had been thrown out of games during the season, Sain asked Tommie to put someone else in charge of the team. Sain would be the logical choice, but he cares only about his pitchers.

While Johnny Sain knows about pitching, he is mostly a motivator. He talks about "selling ideas," and he is a saleman for theories of pitching. He gets hurlers to believe in themselves and their pitches, and he is confident in them.

He spoke of his students in Richmond. "All these guys' physical abilities in Class AAA baseball are the same as the big leagues. But they've got to get the know-how and confidence to add to their physical ability."

But as successful as Johnny has been, he is also one of the most controversial and maligned coaches in the game. Most baseball coaches are faceless individuals who throw batting practice and provide the ego massage for the manager. Sain has strong views on pitching that he will voice, and because of these views, and probably also because of his success, some in the baseball world knock him. Another reason front offices shrug at the mention of Johnny Sain is that he has been known to give players advice during contract time. "Don't ever be afraid to climb those golden stairs and ask," was what Sain told a young Jim Bouton to do when he needed more money.

Bouton swears by Sain, and yet Johnny admitted that he has little knowledge about the knuckleball. "Knuckleball pitchers have a language all their own. I once listened to a conversation between Dutch Leonard and Wilbur Wood, and I learned more that evening than I ever knew before about the knuckler."

What little he claimed to know, he tried to impart to Jim. Sain still believes in Bouton. "He can take adversity. A pitcher doesn't really learn how to pitch until he's hurt his arm, and Jim has learned how to pitch. He's got the game figured out mentally. He's adjusted his mind to using the knuckleball after those years of just being a velocity pitcher."

He was ready to leave, but still he had never really said what he thought of Jim Bouton. He stopped and finally committed himself. "He is sensational as a person. He's always been one of my favorites." And then he added: "Only three people believed Jim Bouton could make it. Ted Turner, Jim Bouton, and myself."

All his comments on pitching, motivation, and selling ideas had been Johnny Sain, the teacher, emphasizing his first point, his opening statement in the interview: "I don't give up on anyone until they give up on themselves."

Johnny Sain had never given up on Jim Bouton.

Sain preached to Jim that there were three things that got batters out: first, velocity; second, movement of the ball; third, location.

It required a man of Johnny's stature, someone Bouton considered ranking up with the angels, to convince Jim that his fast ball had died years ago and would never be resurrected.

During his six weeks as a Richmond Brave, Bouton worked on his knuckleball, palm ball, and a new pitch taught to him by Sain called a "cut fast ball." A "cut fast ball" will never be confused with the high velocity offerings of Jim's youth, but this sharp-breaking pitch gave him another weapon.

With Richmond, Bouton was a nonentity. He was not on the team's active roster and he made ends meet by throwing batting practice for meal money (ten dollars a day in Class AAA). He was a guy Ted Turner wanted to have around, so there he was waiting for yet another opportunity.

The Richmond players would watch Jim run his many sprints and perform a set of strenuous exercises and shake their heads in confusion. To them, Bouton seemed intelligent and a decent person, but he just didn't know how to read a calendar. They pitied him.

Bouton was cognizant of their opinions. That didn't stop him from carrying around his cooler full of health foods or toting his equipment around in a bag labeled "Washington Americans," a remnant of his TV series. Nor was he intimidated by the snickering that inevitably came from the dugout whenever he prepared himself physically each day as if he were getting ready for a World Series game.

During the contests, Jim wasn't in uniform. He wandered through the stands, a lost soul seeking a resting place. When the team traveled the International League circuit, Bouton tagged along to pitch batting practice and tried to find a team in such towns as Columbus, Syracuse, and Rochester that might be interested in acquiring a 39-year-old pitcher.

Most minor league managers would have been uneasy with a former big leaguer and owner's pet like Bouton being around with no apparent purpose. But Tommie Aaron is not like most bush league pilots. The younger brother of the legendary home run hitter, Tommie has a quiet and accepting nature. A man in his position, cursed from birth by being "Hank's little brother," has to take a good deal in order to survive.

Someone with less character never would have followed a god-like brother into baseball. But the summer game is as much a part of Tommie's life as it is Hank's. Tommie was an adroit fielding first baseman with little power who spent a few years in the majors. When people heard the name Aaron, they thought of the long ball, the one big swing of the bat which turns a game around.

"You can't compare Henry and me. I found out a long time ago that I wouldn't be as good a player as he was, but if I let it bother me I wouldn't have stayed around this long," said Tommie. "No two men are alike and nobody understands that more than me."

Generally an easier person to communicate with and get to know, Tommie is slowly working his way out of Henry's huge shadow. Because he lacked a large dose of natural ability, Tommie took time to learn the intricacies of the sport and that is why he is a manager. Hank's little brother has prevailed for five years as a bush league mentor and is now on the threshold of reaching a level that Hank will probably never attain, that of becoming a big league manager.

In fact, everybody in Class AAA is on the doorstep of fulfilling a dream. Many of these athletes have been in the majors and are receiving big league salaries. Their travel and accommodations are usually first class. One can watch an International League game and see no difference between that contest and one played in cities like New York and Atlanta. If there is any one factor that separates a Class AAA player from his major league counterparts, it's confidence. A minor leaguer says, "I think I can do it," while those in the big leagues say, "I've been in this situation before and I succeeded. I know I can do it again."

This was the difference between Jim Bouton and most of the other Richmond pitchers. Bouton had the faith in himself which made success inevitable even if his ability was not on a par with many of the sturdy young hurlers.

But Bouton had no chance to display his confidence or even his knuckleball during his first six weeks with the Richmond Braves. "All I did was throw batting practice, and the guys wouldn't let me throw my knuckleball at them. I just had to throw it up there for them to hit," recalled Jim.

Tommie Aaron was happy to have Bouton around, even if he wasn't exactly sure why he was there. "Jim's a hell of a guy. He'd throw batting practice every day, and that was great because it meant that I didn't have to do it," said Aaron.

Bouton had impressed Tommie in spring training. "He was the top hustler in camp and I had no problems with him in Richmond. He got along with everybody, never missed a bus or caused trouble. Atlanta told me to call them if I had trouble but there was no need. Frankly, I'd rather take a chance with a younger pitcher. The future is with young guys, but Ted Turner wanted Bouton with me and that was fine," explained Aaron.

It was Tommie Aaron who found a way to give Jim the opportunity he had longed for.

The Atlanta Braves were coming to Richmond for an exhibition game. Aaron's team had just suffered through several rugged games in which the members of his pitching staff had all worked. In other words, Tommie needed someone to start against Atlanta.

As would be expected, Bouton volunteered. Tommie Aaron thought for a moment, and said, "Why not." He called the Atlanta front office and proposed that Jim start against the big team; they agreed.

6

The Biggest Game

Jim Bouton was one of the few people who took his start against the Atlanta Braves seriously. Everyone else considered it a farce, part of the festive atmosphere created by Ted Turner.

This was the first time in five years that Atlanta had played an exhibition game in Richmond, and Turner longed to put on a memorable show. The Braves owner wanted to be a part of the game, so he decided to serve as third base umpire.

Richmond General Manager Jon Richardson pulled out all of his promotional tricks. He lined up Hank Aaron and former Baltimore star Brooks Robinson to make appearances. There was also a deal with an oil company whereby tickets for the contest were being sold at half price at gas stations throughout the city.

The Braves organization thought so little of Bouton's comeback that they assigned him number 28, the numeral worn by Seymour Baseball. Seymour Baseball, the team's mascot, is a fellow with a huge plastic baseball for a head who wanders through the stands during the games. Implied in all this hype was a metaphor. Seymour Baseball finally gets his shot at the big leagues in the person of Jim Bouton. The game had the same flavor as the one years before when Bill Veeck had sent a midget up to bat for the St. Louis Browns.

All of this hoopla did little to bolster Bouton's confidence. This contest was a very serious thing to him. The life and death of his baseball career and his dreams were at stake.

"The Richmond game was even more crucial than a World Series game, because if you start a Series game and get shelled, you're still a starter next spring. If I got hit hard, it was all over," said Bouton to a *New Times* reporter.

On the day of the game, Bouton was clearly nervous, feeling more pressure than ever before. "I'm breaking in a new jockstrap for this one," he joked weakly prior to the game.

Jim had every reason to be concerned. The last time he had faced a major league team was eight summers before. His experience in 1977 did not make him believe that he could mow down the Atlanta Braves. Added to all this was the fact that he hadn't pitched competitively during his six weeks in Richmond.

"Obviously, the odds are stacked against me. A lot of people with the Braves would like to see me humiliated so that I'll disappear and they won't look bad if I return to the Big Leagues," said Bouton.

As he dressed, Jim discussed with a *New Times* reporter the possible outcomes of his performance and what they would mean. "First and most likely to happen is that I'll get bombed. That will be the end of my career.

"A second possibility is that I'll pitch great. I pitch something like seven innings, strike out about five guys, give up a run or two, and we beat the Atlanta Braves. Right after the game Ted Turner comes in with a contract. Then I pitch a couple of games with Richmond to get sharp and then move up into the big league's starting rotation.

"The third possibility is that I pitch well enough but nothing super. That's the one I try not to think about because it would leave my future up in the air."

If there was one person on the field who appreciated the ordeal Bouton was undergoing, it was Johnny Sain. "The comeback route is a tough way to make it because you have to be an instant success. Jim's trying to do what no one else has ever done, and he probably has more pressure on him than ever before," noted Sain.

Tommie Aaron had an understanding of the importance of this game to Bouton, too. He also knew how fragile an athlete's ego could be. "I'm planning to pitch him six or seven innings. But I'm not going to let things get out of hand. If they get two or three runs that's fine, but I'm not going to let him get his brains knocked out," said Aaron.

The Bouton family had made the trip to Richmond to see whether or not Dad would be heading home the next day. Their emotions were mixed. None of them wanted to see Jim routed and mentally defeated. Yet, they were lonely and would like him around the house. After a year, it was apparent that this return to baseball and his youth was not something he would easily surrender.

Warming up, Bouton was calling upon all the inner fortitude he warehoused over the years. This was Jim's kind of pressure-filled game, "Warmup Bouton" was getting his chance against the "naturals." At first, his knuckler sauntered up to the plate in a very straight and civilized fashion. That was bad news. Those pitches usually ended up over the fence. Suddenly, Jim discovered he was pressing too hard. He was overthrowing, forcing the pitch. That's the worst way to deliver a knuckleball.

"Then I thought about my situation and realized that this whole thing was going to be a lot of fun, something to tell my grandchildren about. I had talked my way into a game with the Atlanta Braves and I decided that I was just going to enjoy it," said Bouton.

In the stands were more than 13,000 fans. It was an incredible crowd, the product of timely promotions and Bouton's appeal. Just before the National Anthem, most fans were observing Jim warm-up. They also saw Richmond catcher Bruce Benedict battling the ball as if he were trying to swat a fly. The old man was throwing something that was moving.

As Bouton took the mound, Ted Turner gave him a big smile and a wave from third base. It was obvious that Jim still had a fan in Turner.

Jerry Royster was the first batter for Atlanta. He was a fleet infielder who was batting .310 at the time, and Bouton did not want him to reach base and then be a threat to steal off the slow and unpredictable knuckler.

Jim's first offering broke about two feet straight down and landed in the dirt. The next pitch did the same thing, but Bouton wasn't worried. He had his "superknuck," the pitch that made its way to the plate like a drunk weaving around and finally falling down the stairs. It's the kind of pitch that Bouton says "even God couldn't hit."

Two more knuckleballs were delivered to Royster. Each dropped like a clay pigeon shot out of the air and Royster swung and missed them both. Bouton was wild with another knuckler, and the count was three and two.

Not wanting to walk Royster, Jim threw his newest tool, the "cut fast ball." Seeing that the pitch was not a dreaded knuckleball, Royster almost jumped out of the batter's box trying to hit it. At the final second, this offering eluded Royster's bat, breaking just a few inches, and Bouton had a strikeout.

Next Biff Pocoroba grounded to second base, and that brought up Jeff Burroughs, the most feared hitter in the Atlanta lineup. A squat, muscular man who had belted 41 homers in 1977, Burroughs was the kind of hitter who made a nonmoving knuckleball go for what seemed like miles when he made contact.

Employing a combination of palm balls, cut fast balls,

and knucklers, Bouton also induced Burroughs to go down swinging.

Following the first frame, the crowd solidly backed Bouton. Now they and everyone else knew why he had been hanging around for six weeks.

It was the fifth inning and Atlanta had yet to score, Richmond held a 1-0 lead. "Warmup Bouton" was putting them down like the old "Bulldog" used to. Ted Turner kept calling to Tommie Aaron from third base after each inning: "Isn't he something, Tommie?"

His teammates, along with the Atlanta players and executives, were shocked by Jim's success. "After each inning, the guys on the Richmond bench would look at me differently. At first, they thought I was some pathetic old man throwing batting practice, a forlorn character in a way. Now I was sticking it to the Atlanta Braves and they couldn't believe it. I was controlling a game against a major league team, which was something they had always wanted to do," recalled Bouton.

Atlanta finally tallied in the sixth on a walk, a ground ball, and a single. The Braves started the seventh with another hit and a walk. Tommie Aaron saw how tired the 39-year-old hurler was and the manager removed him from the game.

As Bouton walked to the dugout, the 13,000 fans (which represented a $26,000 gate to the Richmond club) were standing and cheering. Jim stopped on his way in and waved his hat triumphantly to the throng.

It was over. Atlanta eventually won the contest 7–3, but that was academic. Bouton left with a 3–1 lead after six innings. He had allowed seven hits, walked three, and fanned seven. He was a success by anyone's standards.

As he undressed in the locker room, Jim was ecstatic. He was talking about pitching until he was 55. He was talking about how he always had believed in himself. He talked so fast and with such delight about what had happened that the reporters couldn't hope to keep up.

Meanwhile, Ted Turner was accepting congratulations from some friends. This game was as much his making as Bouton's. Turner had a hunch, a feeling about some 39-year-old washed-up pitcher that nobody else wanted, and he had been right.

Turner shook Bouton's hand after the game and said, "Don't worry, we'll find a place for you somewhere."

In the stands, Atlanta General Manager Bill Lucas had little to say. He had approved Bouton's release during the spring and was proven wrong by the knuckleballer. "I guess if I was a scout, I'd have to be demoted over this one," explained Lucas.

There still was a problem of just what to do with Bouton. Richmond had a full complement of pitchers, so there was no room in Class AAA. Finally Lucas, Turner, and Hank Aaron decided to send him to Savannah, the Braves' Class AA team in the Southern League.

Bouton happily packed his bags and left the next day. He had won the most important battle of his baseball career and now a new life was beginning.

Part Three
Savannah

7

A Home

Savannah, Georgia, is a town of Spanish moss, century-old trees, and cobblestone streets. It is a place where people sit on porches and drink ice tea and it is the ideal setting for a romantic novel about the Old South.

Many of its residents cast their futures with the sea, serving in that timeless profession of shrimping. A bad season, when few of the seafood delicacies are found in the water, causes concern but few abandon the work of their great-grandfathers.

The town has an accepting nature. When General Oglethorpe brought the first settlers to the area in 1728, the local Indians greeted them warmly.

General Sherman, that Union commander with a fondness for fires and mass destruction, couldn't find it in his heart to so much as light a match in this city where he completed his march to the sea. Sherman saw no reason for violence, since the residents followed the lead of the Indians and permitted the General to set up his headquarters in the best house in town.

It is in this setting that a 39-year-old man, gripping a baseball by his fingertips, became a boy again.

The boy's name is Jim Bouton and he has done quite a few things in his life, but all he ever really wanted to do was play ball and be good at it.

In Savannah, where the daughters of the Confederacy thrive and something isn't considered old unless it goes back before "the war" (the Civil War), Jim Bouton became young again and the people here saw nothing unusual about a middle-aged man wanting to play ball. After all, he really isn't that old, they would say.

Playing ball. The feeling of a game of catch. The joy of pounding a fist into a baseball glove. The smell of bats casted with pine tar. The movements of the body bending, stretching, exerting itself.

To Jim Bouton, it is exhilaration. Playing ball has meant money, fame, and grief. But more than anything else, it has meant the joy of being alive.

Life is never so simple as when it is viewed from a pitcher's mound. A man stands on a small hill with a ball in his hand. He is the conductor of an orchestra of athletes who don't swing into action until he throws the first pitch.

The rules are elementary, written for a child. Baseball is a timeless sport where the foul line runs out into infinity. The game lasts until a winner is discovered. It could take all day or night, but eventually the participants know how they fared.

Success is easy to define. For a pitcher, it's keeping the hitter off base, while the batter strives for just the opposite result. In this game, numbers are important. Three strikes, four balls, nine innings, .300, and 90 feet. In the end, it's the numbers that tell the story and there is no doubt about the outcome.

Ah, if only life were so simple.

It's the childlike qualities of the sport which brought Jim

Bouton to this city. It's the idea of knowing exactly what yields success, what he's expected to do, that brings him out to the mound at Savannah's Grayson Stadium, where it's 95 degrees despite the fact that the sun has set more than two hours before.

Bouton feels the sweat forming under his arms, on his forehead, and at his waist. He licks his upper lip, and it tastes like salt. Even his hands are sweating.

He holds the baseball by his fingertips. A blond-haired kid who just started to shave is standing in the batter's box.

At 39, Bouton has been a ball player, an actor, an author, a television personality, a father watching his children make the same mistakes he did, and a man experiencing all the pressures of middle age.

But standing on that sweltering hill in Savannah, Georgia, Bouton doesn't think about those things. His only concern is throwing his knuckleball past the blond-haired kid.

In Savannah, Jim Bouton is becoming a child, a boy playing ball. He has played this game with time before—in Portland; Knoxville; Durango, Mexico—and lost. But this is timeless Savannah and Bouton has succeeded. The fair-haired boys of the minors would knuckle under to Jim's slow offerings, and never before has the former author felt so good about himself.

Jim Bouton is sweating and making $50,000 less than his usual salary. But that doesn't matter. Nothing matters so long as he is playing ball.

Bouton and the Busher

The arrival of Jim Bouton in Savannah wasn't exactly viewed as the second coming of the Saviour.

Media people found him, as always, interesting and charming. What had become the age-old questions of "Why is Bouton back?" and "Is he writing another book?" all cropped up again.

Astute Savannah fans didn't become overly excited about the newest Brave. They had heard about his debacle with Knoxville of the same Southern League last summer and they, like almost everyone else, weren't sure what he was trying to prove. Many thought he would become another Denny McLain.

McLain was a 31-game winner in 1968 with Detroit. He hurt his arm and spent the waning days of his career in the Southern League, toiling for Knoxville in 1972 with a 2–3 record and a 5.45 ERA. In his final performance in this loop, he was clobbered at Savannah's Grayson Stadium. The degree of the drubbing was so severe that McLain even allowed a home run to the pitcher.

When it came to Bouton, most fans had a cautious curiosity about him. But the presence of a famous former major leaguer in Class AA is almost a guarantee of new interest in a team and at least one above-average crowd.

As for his new teammates, "About half of them were against his coming and the other half really couldn't have cared less," Savannah pitcher Dan Morogiello explained. Like the rest of baseball, the Savannah Braves simply couldn't understand the reasons for Bouton's actions.

"I remember seeing Bouton on the first day of spring training and thinking, 'The old S.O.B. just won't give up.' It was sad, but like a lot of people, I thought he was an old man who should let the younger guys take over," said Savannah relief pitcher Stu Livingstone.

It wasn't just Bouton's presence which aggravated the Savannah players, it was the manner in which he arrived and the roster changes that occurred in order to accommodate him.

Bouton was known as an "executive decision," meaning that Ted Turner and Ted Turner alone decreed his going to Savannah to pitch. Bill Lucas didn't like it. Hank Aaron didn't like it. Minor League Administrator Paul Snyder didn't like it. Almost every athlete in the minor league system didn't like it. Like a South American government where a dictator is all-powerful, a team owner's one whim outweighs all the wishes of those below him.

So Jim Bouton became a member of the Savannah Braves and Bobby Dews, the team's manager, was worried. "Everybody told me there was no way I could come out a winner around Bouton," said Dews, who was convinced that Bouton was just gathering material for another book.

Dews was also the man who had to inform two Savannah pitchers that their status was changing because of Bouton. "Since we had Bouton, I had to tell Vince Titus [a Savannah reliever] that he was being sold to the Mexican League and

Al Pratt [another SavBrave pitcher] that he was being shipped to Greenwood [the Braves' Class A team]. That wasn't a pleasant task, and it was all Bouton's fault," explained Dews.

The veteran Savannah skipper expressed his disgust with the situation to the press. "I have no interest in a 39-year-old pitcher. Ted Turner sent him to me and told me to pitch him. I will, but I don't like it," fumed Dews.

The quote reached the Atlanta front office and Dews received a disciplinary call from the Braves' brass, telling him to shut up and let them make the personnel decisions.

"I was convinced that Bouton was on a lark and doing all this for a wrong, selfish reason. My role is to develop *prospects* and I just didn't see how Jim Bouton fit in that category," said Dews.

Following his initial comments in the press, Dews arrived at the clubhouse the next day wearing a piece of tape over his mouth. He vowed never to say anything about Bouton again.

No matter how hard he tried, Bobby Dews could not comprehend the essence of Jim Bouton.

Bouton had done what Bobby Dews had always longed to accomplish. He was a World Series hero, had fame, money, and luxury. Foremost in Dews' mind was the fact that Bouton was a former big leaguer, a guy who had won twenty games and put in enough time to receive a pension.

A *Sports Illustrated* article on Bouton featured a section on Dews under the heading "The Busher." When you come right down to it, that's exactly what the facts reveal. But Dews and most of those who played for him, including Bouton, believe this label is a misnomer, in the same way the tag "troublemaker" and "old" were hung after Bouton's name.

Dignity and class. Those are the adjectives that come to mind when talking with Dews. One would never view him as a busher. Just fifteen days younger than Bouton, the Savannah manager looks more like a lawyer or a banker than a minor league manager. The size of his car adds to this image. Dews drives a 1971 black Cadillac with more than 91,000 miles on the odometer. Like Dews, the car has covered its share of ground and it's not what they're driving in Atlanta these days, but it has a sense of dignity and class. "It's a good, functional car with a little luxury. The kind they don't make anymore," says Dews.

The native of Edison, Georgia, is a lot like his car. He's a product of the old school but operates quite well in the late 1970's. The son of Bobby Dews, Sr., also a career minor leaguer, he was raised on the diamond. Dews Sr. started in baseball at 16 as a catcher in Class AA and played for another twenty years, never reaching the brass ring of the majors.

"I always went with whatever team my father played for as the club's bat boy from the time I was eight years old," said Dews, whose parents separated when he was in the first grade, after which he lived with his father and grandparents.

As a youngster, he had traveled the same circuits he now visited with Savannah, and showered and dressed in the same clubhouses. "Being in baseball all the time, I never looked at my dad as a father. He was more like a big brother, one of the guys on the team. It was the manager who was more like a father. He set the rules and they came first in my life."

Folks in Edison knew that young Bobby Dews was something special. He was destined to be a ball player like his father, only better. He was going to be a big leaguer.

"People in town sort of took care of me because of my family situation. They would buy me Cokes and things and say that I could pay them back when I was in the majors. Because I was raised in baseball, it was always assumed that I would be a ball player. There was never any discussion about it."

So Dews followed the path set before him. After high school, he was a skinny, 6-foot-1, 145 pounds, and not really ready for professional baseball. Unlike Bouton, he was a natural athlete and excelled on the basketball court, playing a game which he thought would just keep him in shape for baseball. Georgia Tech liked the way Dews performed in a gym and offered him a scholarship.

At Tech, he teamed up with All-American Roger Kaiser to form the backcourt of a Yellow Jackets' squad which won the National Invitational Tournament in New York City.

Meanwhile, he had filled out and refined his diamond skills to the point where the St. Louis Cardinals offered him a $20,000 bonus in 1960. So Bobby left school after his junior year intent on not just becoming a professional; he was headed for the majors.

A shortstop with excellent speed, he had the misfortune of having only an average bat and of being in the same system with stellar infielder Dick Groat. But there was one year when he put it all together, when he did enough to prove his worth and earn a big league chance.

The year was 1964 and Dews batted .277 and swiped 30 bases with Tulsa of the Texas League. "I knew I had been scouted and was sure that some team could use me. But nobody wanted me. I played five more years, but knew it was over right then."

In 1965 the final blow to Dews' dreams occurred when he was hit by a thrown ball in practice and suffered a ruptured spleen. He had an operation and still carries an unsightly eight-inch scar. It took him two years to recover fully, and his speed seemed to have been left on the operating table.

When the sport became a dead end, Dews' grandfather, a prominent lawyer and a state legislator, made him an offer. "After I played ball a few years, I found out that my grandfather really wanted me to be a lawyer. He said I should give baseball five years and if it didn't work, he'd give me his books and get me into a good law school."

There were friends who offered to set him up in business, real estate or insurance. In the off-season, Dews even finished college and picked up a degree in education. But the diploma was really nothing more than something to sit in the attic. His first wife knew that, and she left him because he refused to abandon the game. His life has always been and will always be baseball. After switching to the dugout in 1969, he managed in Lewiston, Cedar Rapids, Sarasota, Modesto, Greenwood, Kingsport, and Savannah.

"It always has been baseball for me. I love it. I'm obsessed. There are a lot of things I would do to make $15,000, but there's nothing I'd rather do than be in the game. My team may be twenty games out in August, but I'm still in the game. Always hoping, believing something will turn things around. I think about it day and night during the season.

"I've been in the minors all my life and I guess that makes me a busher. But I don't think of myself that way. I always wanted to make the big leagues and still do. I know some people are disappointed in me because I haven't made it, but I think I'm good enough to be up there as a coach or manager for somebody."

As a manager, Dews' hero was the volatile Billy Martin. So Bobby gained the reputation as a hothead. One famous tale of his temper still makes the minor league rounds. He was managing in Kingsport at the time and disagreed with a call at third base. The argument raged on and finally Dews became so incensed that he picked up third base, ran into his office with it, and locked the door. His team had to forfeit because the park didn't have any extra bases.

But a change came over him in 1976. He had been calling the signals and arguing with the ferocity of an enraged cougar and was still in Class A after seven summers. Suddenly, he discovered that constantly yelling only made him lose his voice and that tearing up the clubhouse just meant more deductions from his paychecks.

"Every manager I was ever associated with was always a tough guy. I remember one manager who refused to stop the bus to let the players eat after a loss. I thought I had to be that way, too. It took me a while to realize that I should be human. Always shouting was eating me up inside," said Dews.

In 1976 Bobby was remarried to a speech teacher in Albany, Georgia. "His wife settled him down," said Dan Morogiello, who pitched under Dews in three minor league seasons. "She made him be more patient and easygoing, and that made him a better manager."

The old Bobby Dews would never have accepted Jim Bouton on any terms. But the new Bobby Dews was a teacher, a man with a tranquil soul, someone who had stopped attempting to shape his future and now took each day one at a time.

He's still the organization man who will back the sport and his team with the loyalty of a devout priest to his church. He had never read *Ball Four* but had heard from others about it. He knew that he wouldn't like it or its author.

"But I'm a minor league manager whose job it is to get all of my players to the big leagues. I don't care if they send me Frankenstein, I'll do my best to get him up there."

Jim Bouton started as Dews' Frankenstein. By the end of the summer, Bouton was to become his Michelangelo. But in the beginning, Dews was hardly thrilled with his newest acquisition.

Many of Bouton's new teammates viewed the knuckleballer as Frankenstein. They resented him because of what had happened to Pratt and especially to Titus. When a player is exiled to Mexico, it normally means he is dead to American baseball and that his career is over. At the time, Titus had pitched very little, but his ERA was 2.45 and it was believed that he didn't deserve a fate so tragic.

"All of this just made it seem like Bouton was something special, someone better than us, and the guys didn't like it," added Morogiello.

Bouton's enthusiasm also baffled his new colleagues. Thrilled to be part of a team again, he was content just to be around the good-natured profanity of the clubhouse. During the first few weeks, he just listened and felt things. The scraping sound of spikes on the cement floor, the sweet smell of pine tar, and the battle for control of the clubhouse radio between rock, soul, and country music listeners was exhilarating.

What made things even better was the fact that he was back on the road to the majors. He was in Class AA, a starting pitcher just a few good games away from his goal. Furthermore, his ultimate boss, Ted Turner, was rooting for him to make it.

"Jim was all fired up when he first got here. I mean, he was so happy just to be back that he would take all the routine fielding drills really seriously and he'd give the other guys hints which they really didn't want to hear. Finally, we just told him, 'Jim, we know what to do.' That settled him down, but the guys wondered about him even more," recalled Stu Livingstone.

Bouton was caught up in the romantic aspects of his new endeavor. He kept telling the press things like, "It's just great to be on a bus going to some small town for a new adventure."

To him, it was wonderful to be back in the mainstream of baseball. It was marvelous to be struggling to make the majors with guys like Bobby Dews, Stu Livingstone, and Dan Morogiello, even if they didn't think so.

9

Becoming a Winner

As Jim Bouton looked around Savannah's Grayson Stadium, he realized that his choreography had surpassed his pitching. When one thought about it, there was no logical reason for him to be there. Baseball has no use for 39-year-old minor league pitchers who throw knuckleballs or laser beams. The whole thing was simply incredible, a miracle.

But the miracles were just beginning, and Bouton didn't have much time for reflection. He was due to pitch against the Nashville Sounds in just five hours. Now he had to meet the media to sell some tickets for the game by giving out interviews.

Bouton looked closely at the park as he talked. Like so many of the large, public facilities across the country, Grayson Stadium is a remnant of the Depression. It's a middle-aged woman in need of a bath and a little makeup. One would never mistake it for a major league stadium.

76

Actually, it's a park or field in the manner of Fenway or Ebbets. The grandstand runs from first to third base and is entirely screened in by chicken wire. Folding chairs compose the box seats, and the fans situated there can hear whatever infield chatter is being uttered. The outfield walls are plastered with signs advertising radio stations, headache cures, hamburgers, dry cleaners, and an ice company.

This was Bouton's first trip to Grayson Stadium. He didn't last long enough during his initial stint in the Southern League to appear in the Georgia Port City.

He walked onto the field and saw that the park was similar to several he had passed through during the years. Behind the box seats were aging, wooden benches for the $1.75 general admission fans. To Bouton there was nothing very notable about the grandstand.

Then his eyes went out to right field. It was 310 feet down the line, and curved sharply out, making the power alley 395. A good place for a pitcher, Bouton thought. The deepest part of the field was right-center (410 feet) while dead center stood 400 feet away.

As Bouton looked at left field, a lump formed in his throat. The bleachers there seemed to be right behind the shortstop. The sign on the left-field foul line said 290. A guy could hit a 291-foot homer in this park. Bouton thought of the 18 homers he had allowed in eight games at Knoxville last year. With a porch like this, he might give up 80. There was every reason for a knuckleball pitcher to worry. A half-swing by a strong right-handed hitter could knock the ball out of Grayson Stadium.

With the media pacified and his tour of the park concluded, Jim walked into the clubhouse.

In *Ball Four*, Bouton had said that the bats in the Tacoma dressing room of the Class AAA Pacific Coast League were stored in garbage cans. He felt this was a perfect metaphor for the minors. Well, the Savannah Braves didn't even have trash cans for their bats. The players just kept them in their cramped locker-like stalls.

Upon entering the clubhouse, the smell of sweat, tobacco juice, and pine tar immediately attacks the nose. There's no air conditioning and the humid Savannah climate makes the cracked cement floors and walls feel damp. The room is painted a faded army green. When one sees a few cockroaches scurrying across the floor, some the size of small mice, there is no doubt that this is the minor leagues. The surroundings are dreary, thanks to the ancient fluorescent lighting system with bulbs that were last washed during the Roosevelt administration. But these rooms contain more hopes and dreams than any area of its size in Savannah.

It is the players who give this place life, just as a smiling face and a sincere handshake make a stranger feel comfortable. During the season, the room is filled with guys laughing and engaging in the profane insult games that athletes so love to play. On a professional baseball team, men use the type of foul banter the rest of society reserves for poker games and other informal gatherings of men. The locker room is a place where men act like young teenagers still growing accustomed to their manhood.

At 39, there was no question about Bouton's manhood. In fact, many felt he was experiencing male menopause and the middle-age doldrums. But he didn't have time to consider his psychological state. His main concern was getting the Nashville Sounds out.

Once again Jim proved to be an excellent drawing card. The Savannah Braves came up with an original promotion by admitting free anyone with a copy of *Ball Four*.

Right before the game, Bouton was nervous and scared. It was the same feeling he had had before the game with Atlanta. The stands were filled with 3,182 fans, 2,000 above the regular season average.

Bouton received a warm hand, but nothing compared to the embracing, enthusiastic responses he would elicit later in the summer. The fans had come to laud Bouton if he did well, but a disaster would bring a thunderous boo. For the moment, they were withholding their judgment, as was the rest of the baseball world.

The temperature was in the low 90's and Bouton was sweating profusely before he even threw his first pitch.

It was May 19 and Nashville and Savannah were both slogging at a .500 pace. This game meant little to the pennant race. But to Bouton it was everything. This situation wasn't as crucial as the one a week earlier in Richmond, where he had to do well or go home. There would be a few more starts for Jim regardless of the outcome. Yet, there was a dire need to show his new teammates that he belonged. He had to make a profound statement to demonstrate that he wasn't a gimmick.

So the pressure and urgency were there. Bouton felt it and liked the setting. There was nothing in television that could compare with it.

The lead-off batter was Nashville's Rick Duval. Bouton fed him a stream of knuckleballs, the slowest offerings Duval had seen in some time in this league dominated by hard throwers in their early 20's. The count ran to three and two and Bouton lobbed a knuckler that dropped like a duck shot in midair. Duval helplessly waved at it for strike three and the crowd exploded. Bouton then induced the next two hitters to ground weakly to third and the first inning was over.

His teammates gave Jim a 2–0 lead as he started the second frame. It was going to be Richmond all over again. Bouton felt that same "magic" which had vaulted him past the Atlanta Braves. The spell disappeared abruptly as Nashville's Tim Doerr rapped Bouton's first offering of the inning into the left-field porch.

Once again, Jim was worried. He knew that there'd be trouble with that short fence. Nonetheless, he managed to blank the Sounds over the next two innings and had a 2–1 lead entering the fourth.

By this point, things were progressing quite well. Already Bouton had proved that he wasn't just lucky against the Atlanta Braves. He had something and that something was working against Nashville. The first two batters were retired easily.

Tim Doerr was again at the plate. Bouton pitched him cautiously, recalling his home run back in the second. But Doerr ripped a double to left-center. Then George Weicker squarely met a knuckler and deposited it over the nearby left-field fence. Jim fanned Greg Dahl to end the inning, but he was trailing 3–2. There was no room to relax, not with that left-field porch standing ominously over his right shoulder.

Savannah scored in the fourth and fifth innings, taking a 4–3 lead. Then Bouton became the "Bulldog." It was "stomach time," and he relied on his inner fortitude as much as anything else to carry him in the last four innings. It was moments like these which made him seem miraculous, better than other mortals. He was doing what couldn't be done.

After seven innings, he was tired and Dews saw it.

"You want out?" asked Dews.

"Nah, I'll do it. I'm still strong," replied Bouton.

Right off, Jim didn't want to be pinned with the label of being too old to go the distance. "I could have gone out after seven. I had a 5–3 lead and a win pretty much locked up. This was only the second game I had pitched in two months, so I was tired. But I just had to finish," said Bouton.

As he took the field in the eighth, it was clear Bouton had captured the crowd. They cheered his every pitch and responded to the way he dashed on and off the diamond, backed up bases, and displayed more hustle than most of his teammates.

The Savannah Braves sat in semi-shock. They had expected Bouton to be routed, especially after allowing those early inning homers. Like the Richmond players, they had viewed Jim as a pathetic old man.

Well, the old man was in command. Suddenly, Nashville just wasn't hitting the ball hard any more and the "old geezer" seemed to be growing stronger.

"You could have put the emotions of the team about Bouton on a graph. Each inning he got them out, his stock went up. When he gave up those homers, the bottom dropped out," said Stu Livingstone.

The players and fans began to realize that something special was happening, something that might not take place again for a long, long time. They were watching a man beat all the odds, outrun a calendar, and do what others would never even have dared dream possible. The experience was almost supernatural.

Bouton finished the game with a 5–3 victory. He had struck out eight, the most he would all year, hadn't walked a single batter, and had allowed five hits. More important, he had won the grudging respect of those who opposed him and had gained the admiration of the fans and some of the players.

"Frankly, I didn't know what to expect when Bouton first came here. I thought I would have to remind him about backing up bases and things like that," said Dews. "But he's fundamentally sound and a hustler. He inspired the guys. He's no prima donna."

Inspiration was the correct word for the reaction of the team behind him in the field. He received probably the best defense of any Savannah pitcher. The reason was that Bouton worked fast, which kept the defensive players from growing bored, and he was an adroit fielder.

So Jim Bouton had found his youth in Savannah. He was a little boy playing ball, and even better, he was a winner. Obviously, not all the games would go as smoothly as this one had, but it was indicative of what lay ahead.

10

"Two Wild and Crazy Guys"

One of the problems facing Savannah Manager Bobby Dews was to find a roommate for Bouton. Dews didn't think anybody would want to live on the road with the enigmatic 39-year-old.

He gathered the players together and asked who would be willing to take on Bouton. There was a lot of grumbling, with people saying things like, "I don't want to be in his next damn book" or "I don't even like having him around, much less living with him."

Finally, pitcher Roger Alexander said, "I'll take him."

The room was quiet. Everyone stared at Alexander. Then reliever Stu Livingstone said, "What do you want to room with that clown for?"

"He's all right. I kinda like him," said Alexander.

"Look, you don't need him. He doesn't even belong

here. He's just writing another book," countered Livingstone.

"I'll take him. You guys shouldn't worry about Bouton. If some 39-year-old guy is going to beat you out, you're in trouble," concluded Alexander.

"You'll be sorry," said Livingstone.

Roger Alexander was one of Savannah's most respected pitchers. At Bouton's arrival, he had a 7–0 record and a 0.57 ERA. He was the Southern League's premier hurler. His teammates were surprised to see that an athlete obviously on the way up was willing to take a chance on being sidetracked by Bouton.

"He'll only hurt you," said one player.

But Roger Alexander had been fascinated with Bouton since reading *Ball Four* in junior high.

"The book really got me interested in baseball. It made me want to be a player and I always wanted to meet Jim Bouton," said Alexander.

Unlike Bouton, Alexander didn't collect autographs and baseball cards as a youngster. "Before I read the book, I was passive about baseball. But the book made the players seem human and the game fun. Then I decided to be a ball player," added Alexander.

At 5-feet-10, 170 pounds, Alexander looks quite like Bouton from a distance. A prep star in Norman, Oklahoma, he threw fairly hard and had an excellent curve ball. In 1973, the Milwaukee Brewers were impressed and drafted him in the third round.

Alexander began asking questions about Bouton. Many of those who had been his hero's teammates just said, "That bastard!" and left it at that.

Roger is one of the few players ever traded for a man who later became his boss. He was shipped by Milwaukee to Atlanta, along with Dave May, for aging superstar Hank Aaron. Aaron played the final two years of his illustrious career in the Beer City and returned to Atlanta as the Braves Minor League Director, with Alexander being one of the players under his control.

Meanwhile, Alexander was pitching unspectacularly. He spent three seasons in Class AA before being promoted to Richmond in 1977. With the Braves Class AAA team he was 5–10 with a 4.27 ERA.

In the spring of 1978, he was prepared to go to Richmond again and had been working out with that team. On the final day of camp, Alexander was told by Aaron that Savannah would be his destination instead. The demotion depressed him, but Alexander had no idea that he'd be teamed with his old idol.

There were a number of similarities between Bouton and Alexander which helped compose a solid foundation of a friendship. For both of them, this summer was the pivotal point in their athletic careers. At 24, Alexander was at the crossroads. This was his fourth season in Class AA and he had to establish himself as a big winner.

Like Bouton, who was fighting the "too old" label, Alexander had a tag he was trying to shake. He was considered nothing more than a "career minor leaguer." It was believed by many scouts that he lacked the velocity to be a major leaguer.

Actually, Roger didn't expect to spend much time with Bouton. "I thought a phone call from them telling me I was moving up was coming any minute," recalled Alexander, who was leading the loop in wins, innings pitched, strikeouts, and earned run average.

Despite the credentials, the phone never rang with the good news.

"I just couldn't believe it. Frankly, I had never seen a pitcher who was doing as well as I did when I won my first seven games," added Alexander.

The roommates discussed his situation. Bouton talked about the faceless "they" who make the decisions about athletes, determining who was a prospect, who was too old, and who was just another body.

"There are two ways to fight a label," Bouton told Alexander. "Pitch so well that they can't ignore you, and get the word out to the press. You have to be a salesman for yourself."

So Roger began giving interesting quotes about how he was treated shabbily by the front office by being sent to Savannah and how he was out to show "everyone that they made a mistake." Like Bouton, he kept his statistics on the tip of his tongue.

At first, Bouton and Alexander weren't closer than any of the roommates on the SavBraves. One of the first things that caught Roger's attention was the media, which followed Bouton everywhere, and the way Jim could patiently spout off his saga several times a day.

"You have to deal with reporters. There'll be a lot more than this in the big leagues," said Bouton.

Roger could see the similarities between himself and Bouton. "Both of us were older than the rest of the guys and we both were finding things out about ourselves. Jim needed a goal in his life and he had to be alone in order to sort things out. As for myself, I had to find out if I was going to be a mediocre pitcher for the rest of my life or if I could be something better," said Alexander.

The major topic of conversation was pitching and the proper mental approach.

"You gotta believe in yourself," Bouton would tell him. "Then you can pitch with your stomach during those times when nothing else is working."

Alexander watched Jim closely in his next few starts. He saw a 39-year-old man with just an average knuckleball and the velocity of a softball pitcher retire young, talented prospects. There was no logical explanation for the occurrence.

Meanwhile, things were going wrong for Roger. His teammates had stopped hitting behind him, supplying him with only nine runs in his next seven starts. He was still pitching admirably, but the losses were piling up. Soon his record was 7–6, and Alexander had a feeling that he just might be that bush league hurler "they" said he was.

But Bouton kept telling him about "pitching with your stomach. Guts mean so much in this game. It's what's in your heart that's important."

In Alexander's heart was a void where self-confidence should have been. Bouton reminded him about the power of a positive approach, of knowing you'll succeed. Roger saw Bouton win with little more than his psyche because he believed in pitching with his stomach.

When it comes to the subject of pitching, Bouton makes Norman Vincent Peale sound like a pessimist. Alexander listened, learned, and then the pair practiced what they preached.

An example of this occurred when the team was starting a twelve-hour all-night bus trip from Memphis to Charlotte. Bouton and Alexander were scheduled to pitch a doubleheader there the next day.

"Listen, Rog," said Bouton, "Here's what we're going to do. We're gonna stay up all night, talk and have a good time, and then go out and beat those bastards with no sleep."

The common practice for starting pitchers the night before a game was to battle the bumps and awkward bus seats for a few hours of sleep. Usually they would adopt a foul mood and order those around them to shut up.

"We turned the whole thing into a game," recalled Bouton. "Staying up all night was an added challenge. It made things more interesting."

So they talked and laughed as the headlights and neon signs zipped by. Soon they were in Charlotte and Alexander took the mound, firing a six-hit shutout. Bouton followed with a one-hitter. It was then that Alexander knew what it meant to pitch with his stomach.

"Once you've done it, you can call on it again and again. You know it's there," said Alexander.

A week later they teamed up in another doubleheader, used the same tactics on the bus ride the night before, and came away with another double victory.

All of this served to strengthen the bond between the roommates, but it was their off the field antics which made them close friends.

Jim Bouton wasn't the only SavBrave with major league experience. Don Collins was a left-handed hurler with Atlanta in 1977 and had a 3–9 record with a 5.42 ERA. He started 1978 with Atlanta but was soon shipped to Richmond (where he was 1–6) and finally landed in Savannah.

A third-round draft choice, Collins was accustomed to the big leagues and big money. The Savannah setting galled him and he was out to spend only a few months in the bushes until his elbow trouble cleared up.

Generally a moody person, Collins wasn't very popular with his Savannah teammates. His negative attitude at being stuck in Savannah also carried over to them. Collins resented the publicity Bouton was receiving. Bouton knew this and enjoyed going out of his way to be friendly with the press when Collins was within earshot.

The date was June 14, one day before the major league trading deadline. Bouton and Alexander were standing around in the outfield during batting practice.

"Hey, Rog. I got an idea. Let's trade Don Collins to the New York Mets," said Bouton.

"What are you talking about?" asked Alexander.

"The trading deadline is here and I say that we create a bogus deal, sending Collins to the Mets. It's a big league joke and we gotta do it right," explained Bouton.

"Okay," said Alexander. "What've you got in mind?"

"First we have to create a trade that someone with Collins's ego would swallow. There's got to be a number of players involved to make it realistic," added Bouton.

The deal they invented had Collins, Atlanta catcher Biff Pocoroba, and shortstop Pat Rockett heading to New York for All-Star pitcher Pat Zachary and infielder Tim Foley.

At the time, Bouton was being featured on the "Today Show." An old friend of Jim's, Today reporter Eric Burns, helped with the prank and they soon managed to have Collins thinking he was headed for the Big Apple. Here's how it happened:

1. Bouton asked Burns to call Collins the following morning asking the southpaw for an interview once he arrived in New York. Burns did and told Collins of the trade.

Burns asked Collins if the Mets had contacted him yet. Collins immediately fell for the prank and replied, "Not yet."

2. Collins then called his friends and parents informing them of his fate. He told his teammates of the deal and said that he needed to get an $8,000 car and a new set of clothes since "nobody goes to the Big Apple without a new suit."

3. As the afternoon approached, Alexander became fearful that Collins was catching on. So he left Collins a note saying that a reporter from the New York *Daily News* called and said that he wanted to talk to Collins about the trade. Collins waited in his motel room for the remainder of the afternoon, not even going out for lunch, hoping the unnamed reporter would call back.

4. Finally it was time to go to the ball park and Collins had yet to hear anything. Another note was slipped in his locker, this one saying that the Mets' General Manager, Joe McDonald, had called and would call Collins later.

5. Collins went to Braves Manager Bobby Dews with the note and said that he shouldn't play. Dews said he hadn't heard anything about the trade. Collins also called back his parents and friends saying he was heading to New York for certain.

6. After the game, Collins was trying to get a flight out of Montgomery. Finally, Bouton and Alexander decided that things were getting a little out of hand. They informed him of the prank in a highly professional manner.

7. Bouton taped a message, like a radio bulletin, onto the track of his own country music tape player. The message, heard by the entire team in the clubhouse, said that, "Fishermen Jim Bouton and Roger Alexander caught a tuna fish yesterday . . ." and recalled all the details of the deal.

Bouton then leaked the joke to the Savannah press and it was picked up by *The New York Times*, who dropped Roger Alexander's name from the whole affair.

Collins was furious and humiliated. He refused to talk to Bouton or the local press for months afterward.

"The Don Collins joke really brought us close together.

We really got to know each other after that," recalled Alexander.

Alexander and Bouton started calling themselves "Two Wild and Crazy Guys" like a television comedy duo. They pulled several more pranks, including planting fireworks in the dugout of the Nashville Sounds which ignited at the start of the "Star Spangled Banner" on July 4th. When the explosion occurred, Bouton and Alexander watched from the bullpen.

As their relationship grew, they reinforced each other during hard times. After dropping six straight games, Alexander righted himself by winning three of his last four to have a 10–7 record and a 1.87 ERA at midseason. He was named to start the Southern League All-Star game. Working with two days' rest, Roger pitched a pair of scoreless innings against the big team and was voted the game's MVP. Following the contest, he was promoted to Richmond.

Bouton and Alexander remained in close contact throughout the year, talking at least once a week on the telephone. They were more than old roommates, they became lasting friends.

Bouton and Management

The game was over, but Jim Bouton was not in the clubhouse. As the grounds crew worked on the field and a light mist began to fall, Bouton stalked to the concession stand. He went to the back door and called to a man opening a can of beer. Jim was perturbed.

"Dammit, Dave. I don't mind working on the mound, but you've got to have some tools for me to do it. Don't you realize that those kids out there don't even have a pickax or a pointed shovel. How the hell can I fix the mound if I don't have any tools?"

Bouton was scheduled to pitch the next night. Ever since arriving in Savannah, he worked the night before his starts, digging out the mound to fit his specifications. The man listened as Bouton raged, then followed Jim back to the field to see if perhaps somewhere in the grounds keeper's room there were the proper tools.

The man Bouton had gone to was Dave Fendrick, general manager of the Savannah Braves. He is 29, with a tall, angular build and a friendly, open face. He has been a minor league general manager for five years, the last three in Savannah.

Fendrick searched through the grounds keeper's room but came up with none of the items Bouton desired. He walked out to the mound with a rounded shovel for Bouton and the two of them tried to do a little work, but the shovel would not cut the hard red clay. Bouton returned to the clubhouse and Fendrick went back to his office.

For Dave Fendrick the grounds crew was one of the continuing problems of running a minor league baseball team. He had gone through six different grounds keepers that season, and most of the people he now had working on the field were just young teenagers. The City of Savannah is responsible for supplying a man during the day, and they sent over an ever-changing collection of laborers. At night Dave had to do the hiring.

The Atlanta Braves is the only major league organization that owns all its minor league clubs. The other major league teams generally have working agreements with a minor league team, the big clubs supplying the players while a local operator takes care of all the other expenses. But Atlanta has traditionally owned its own teams, and its method of supervising these teams is with a budget. No one in the Atlanta front office has ever run a minor league club, and each spring the major league controller, an accountant, sets the budget for the individual teams. The amount allotted for a grounds crew is low, very low, and Dave Fendrick had to content himself with hiring those who were neither very professional nor very competent. Ten dollars a night would not attract much more.

Before the 1978 season opened, Fendrick was 90 percent certain this would be his last as a minor league general manager. He was not looking forward to the petty hassles that built up and finally overwhelmed one. Then Bouton came and the season changed. He had been aware that

Bouton was at spring training with the Braves, but then he lost sight of the ex-major leaguer and heard nothing until the exhibition game at Richmond. The following day he received a phone call from Atlanta General Manager Bill Lucas. Bouton was coming to Savannah.

"Nothing like that had ever happened to me in minor league baseball. Once the announcement came that we were getting Bouton and he was starting on May 19, the phone calls never stopped," said Fendrick. "There were calls from all over the United States and Canada. *Sports Illustrated* called to say they were covering the game, and AP sent its man in from Atlanta. It was a whole new experience. All of a sudden I was having to make decisions like whether or not we would allow TV in the locker room. Before that we never had TV wanting to film anything.

"If Bouton hadn't come to Savannah, it would have been just another season. Now we had something that promoted itself. People were actually calling up to reserve tickets to see the Savannah Braves."

There are good minor league cities and bad minor league towns, with Savannah probably ranking somewhere in the middle. But prior to coming to Savannah, Fendrick had been in some of the worst.

There is no direct route to becoming a minor league general manager, and each of the 100 of these men in the country has a different story of how he obtained his position. It is always chance, fate, or simply good or bad luck.

Fendrick probably had more of a professional background than most, for he has a Master's degree in Sports Administration from Ohio University, one of the first and better schools with this type of program. These colleges teach virtually nothing that is helpful in baseball's minor leagues, but in the last half dozen years a good portion of jobs have gone to graduates of Sports Administration courses around the country.

Dave graduated from the Master's program at OU in 1973, and after an internship at San Diego State in the sports information department, he went to work for the Columbus

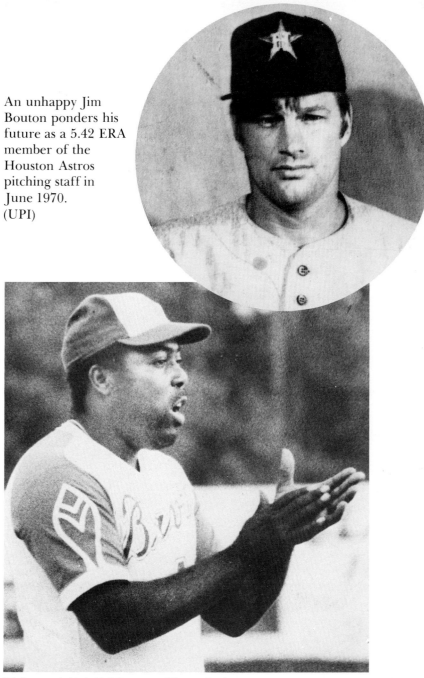

An unhappy Jim Bouton ponders his future as a 5.42 ERA member of the Houston Astros pitching staff in June 1970. (UPI)

Richmond (AAA) Manager Tommie Aaron. (*Savannah News*, Steve Woodford)

Savannah Braves (AA)
Manager Bobby Dews.
(*Savannah News*, Bob Morris)

Chicago White Sox owner Bill Veeck. "I gave Bouton a
chance because no one else would." (UPI)

Atlanta Braves owner Ted Turner and Jim Bouton felt they understood one another. (Wide World Photos)

The Bouton family at Savannah's Grayson Stadium: (L to R) Laurie (11), Bobbie Bouton, Michael (14), and David (13). (*Savannah News*, Bob Morris)

Pitching for the Atlanta Braves (AA). He had a 12-9 record with a 2.77 ERA and twelve complete games during the 1978 regular season. (*Savannah News*, Bob Morris)

Jim Bouton towels himself before taking the mound for the Atlanta Braves against the Los Angeles Dodgers in his return to the majors after an eight-year absence.
(Wide World Photos)

Jim Bouton tips his hat to the Atlanta crowd during his big
league return against the Dodgers. Though he held the Dodgers
hitless for over three innings, he lost and had to be
relieved in the fifth. (Wide World Photos)

"Bouton Beats the Giants" reads the wire service caption, "San Francisco, September 14. Right-hander Jim Bouton of the Atlanta Braves, whose last major league victory was on July 11, 1970, against the Giants, is pictured in action Thursday at Candlestick Park in San Francisco, where he pitched the Braves to a 4 to 1 victory over the San Francisco Giants." (Wide World Photos, 1978)

Barons professional football team of the Central Football League. The team folded shortly thereafter, and Fendrick was without a job.

The fates may or may not have been with him when a friend came back from the winter baseball meetings in Houston in 1973 bearing the news that there were three minor league baseball jobs available. Fendrick, who had written all the major league owners earlier, again started mailing letters.

Dave Fendrick had never been to a minor league baseball game before this time, much less ever seen a minor league park. He had grown up in the big league cities of Cleveland and Chicago and was aware of the minors only as a place that major leaguers went when they weren't doing well. A week after sending out his letters, Fendrick received a call from Pat McKernan, president of the Gastonia Rangers of the Western Carolinas League.

McKernan asked Fendrick if he would like to be the general manager of the Gastonia club. Fendrick's reply was honest. "I really know nothing about minor league baseball. I have no experience."

McKernan's answer was equally honest. "I can send any donkey to Gastonia to run that club." Dave Fendrick became McKernan's donkey.

McKernan, however, failed to mention that the reason he needed a general manager was that he was in the process of selling the club. A week later there was a new owner, Fred Nichols of New Haven, Connecticut, who had never been in baseball before. Nichols stayed in New Haven and Fendrick was left in Gastonia with no one to guide him.

Gastonia, North Carolina, is a textile town of about 35,000 people some 25 miles west of Charlotte. There are many positive things that might be said about Gastonia. However, in professional baseball the information on Gastonia was simple: it was the "pits," the worst city in the game. Gastonia stories were legend, and every ball player or official who went there had his own. Few were exaggerated. At that time, the lights in Gastonia's Sims Legion Park were considered the dimmest in baseball, and more than once an outfielder would dive, miss a fly ball, but quickly pick it up, and hold it over his head, as the umpire signaled "out." In the far reaches of the outfield, it was impossible to see the ball from the infield.

But it wasn't the lights, or the infield that looked like a collection of uneven ruts, or the dirty wooden stands that made Gastonia so infamous. It was the fans. There were not many, perhaps 300 on a good night, but their reputation for being nasty and vicious was well-founded. One umpire carried a loaded pistol when he was given a Gastonia game to call, and many visiting teams had to run to their bus with bats swinging to protect themselves from the crowd.

Dave Fendrick personally became aware of this situation on a night when the umpires had made several calls that had gone against the home team. Twenty minutes after the game, most of the fans were still in the park, crowding around the entrance to the umpires' dressing room. With the general manager's office next door, many of the rocks aimed at the umpires quarters pounded on his door. Finally, Fendrick had to go to the umpires room and personally escort them to their car as the fans followed throwing rocks. The next day, one of the umpires quit and returned home to take a job as a patrolman on the New York City Police Force. He preferred the relative quiet of the big city streets to umpiring in Gastonia.

But Fendrick learned, chiefly by trial and error, and by the season's end, he had become a competent general manager. He did make a few mistakes. One was a greased pig contest where the pig refused to run in the outfield and was promptly squashed by about 100 screaming kids. The dazed animal was mercifully taken under the stands, where it then decided to do its bit, and for two hours it dashed around under the bleachers and through the concession stands as ball park employees helplessly pursued it.

In the low minors, the general manager's job is not year-round, and on September 1, with the season over, Fendrick was out of work. The club had lost about $8,000, the Texas Rangers refused to put another team in Gastonia, and

Dave started looking for another job. His first year's performance, or endurance, had not gone unnoticed, and the following winter he was hired by the Atlanta Braves to run their Greenwood, South Carolina, club of the same Western Carolinas League. Greenwood as a town was little better than Gastonia, although the fans were more subdued, and the next year Fendrick was promoted to Savannah.

When the word came that Bouton was coming to Savannah, Fendrick had mixed emotions. His first thought was that the Braves were being prostituted for another book. Said Fendrick: "How could Bouton lose? If he pitches well and gets to the big leagues, he's got it made; if he bombs out and writes another book, he's got it made then, too."

But when Bouton arrived in Savannah, he immediately won Fendrick over. "Anything you want me to do, Dave, that's why I'm here."

In the minors, as in the majors, it is often difficult to get players to make public relations appearances, and here was a player, probably the most famous in the minor leagues, volunteering. As Fendrick talked to Bouton, he became convinced the man simply wanted to pitch, be it in Savannah, Durango, or wherever. Then, with the press and fan reaction and an opening with Bouton pitching before 3,182 fans, triple the normal average, Fendrick became a Bouton man.

In the weeks that followed, the front office started scheduling Bouton for appearances. He went to a local book store, a radio station, a baseball camp, and spoke at a civic club. He was always willing and gracious and was definitely an asset to the front office operation.

Then a change came over Bouton. To put it simply, he started winning. He was proving he could pitch in Class AA; now working in the minors, just throwing a baseball in organized competition, was no longer the dream. The Bouton vision now was to return to the big leagues, and relations with the minor league front office started to sour. He began to demand more and more, all relatively minor requests, but the unspoken refrain was there: "I did you favors, now you should repay."

It came to a head at the start of an eight-day road trip for the team. Fendrick arrived at the office one morning after the team had left, and there on the door was a note from Jim. It requested him to take Bouton's car to the shop to be fixed while they were on the road.

At face value, it was a minor request, and Fendrick had two assistants who could have easily completed the errand. But the position and authority of a minor league general manager are fragile. He does not pay the team—the checks come from the major league club—and it is difficult to demand anything of a player even though technically the general manager is the boss. The players know their job is determined by the major league farm director, not the minor league executive. Now, a player was putting a note on the door, acting as if the general manager was a "go-for" for Jim Bouton. Fendrick was furious.

The next day Bouton called and asked about his request. Fendrick replied that he was not Bouton's "personal errand boy" and the two had heated words. Bouton brought up that he had spoken to a civic club and in New York he would be paid $1,500 for that.

"As a human being," Bouton told Fendrick, "I would think you would return the favor." The two continued with the argument, and Bouton accused Fendrick of being like all front office people, interested only in money and not people.

When Jim returned, he came into the office and apologized, saying that both of them were wrong, and Fendrick mumbled that he had forgotten about it. But he hadn't, and he was convinced it was part of the Bouton modus operandi. He thought the pitcher needed to be at odds with management (he was a perennial holdout with New York), be it a lowly Class AA general manager, a major league executive, or a national network executive. He felt that Bouton created these situations.

"Hell, if Timothy Leary were general manager of this ball club, Bouton would accuse him of being a conservative stuffed shirt," said Fendrick.

After that incident, relations between the office and Bouton were cool, and there were no more requests for Bouton to make appearances.

Even with this, Fendrick was a Bouton fan. He said it was difficult not to root for the guy when he was out there pitching, and as general manager, he above all others recognized what the pitcher had done for him financially. Jim Bouton had made the year his most memorable in baseball. For this Dave was grateful.

It was August when Fendrick was interviewed, and he sat in the stands and looked out at the field as he talked about the year. With the eighteen-hour days, he was tired, and he definitely now was quitting at the end of the season. He had already informed the Atlanta front office.

"I'm stale. I've got to get out. I've got to see how badly I'm hooked on baseball. I need to see if I can handle a 9-to-5 job. I don't know what I'll do, but I'll try something.

"You know, what gets to you are the games. It's the responsibility. If anything goes wrong, the problem is all yours. If a ball comes through the screen and hits a fan, or if something spoils in the concession stand, or if a fan gets mugged in the john, the problems all come to you. And there is no way you can prepare for them, because you're never sure where they're going to crop up.

"Sure, I've got people responsible in each area, but if the situation really gets sticky, they know they can always throw it to me, and I have to handle it. As Truman said, the buck stops here. And after you come in and work an eight-hour day, then the game starts and you've got four or five more hours of real responsibility. And no one, not the players, not the press, not the fans, can really appreciate what you have to go through. And with 72 home games, it all comes to me.

"The thing is, Atlanta never calls to tell you you're doing a good job or calls to ask if there is anything they can do to help. The only time the front office calls is when something is fouled up, and then they're calling you on the carpet. It really makes you paranoid."

Dave Fendrick thinks of himself as an average guy, a guy who likes to drink beer and go out and have a good time. He says he is not intelligent and has to work and do things twice before he is sure they are right. Jim Bouton will tell you that Dave Fendrick never did learn how to promote properly. The numbers back Bouton up, as Savannah's season attendance dropped by 11,000, despite the presence of Bouton and a pennant-winning team.

Like so many men Bouton encountered during his minor league venture, Dave Fendrick was just worn down and discouraged by the elements confronting him. After a few years, the bushes was a depressing place. Even Jim Bouton realized that. That's why he had to perform superbly, to avoid becoming overwhelmed like Dave Fendrick.

12

Struggling

Above all else, Jim Bouton feared mediocrity. A string of strong performances like this opener against Nashville would hasten his arrival in Atlanta. After a few shellings, he might have to quit and salvage things by writing about the venture as an interesting failure, like those who tried for years to ride balloons across the Atlantic to Europe.

But neither of these things occurred. Jim turned out to be nothing more than an average Class AA pitcher. He was as good as he was bad, and it all hinged on the unpredictable knuckler, which proved to be truly a fickle woman.

He had been with the team for a month and had a 4–4 record. His teammates gained respect for his hustling style and more than a few envied his excellent physique.

"A lot of guys resented the fact that he worked so hard. He'd run sprints, do 40 sit-ups, and take extra fielding drills.

99

Some of them thought he was trying to show them up," recalled Livingstone.

Bouton was enjoying his demanding pregame routine. It was all part of the experiences he had longed for during those years under the bright lights of a television studio.

An example of just how much Bouton enjoyed being back in baseball occurred in a home game against Charlotte. It was the eighth inning and the score was knotted at 3–3. Bouton was coaching first base, a duty he, along with several other players, filled throughout the season. Minor league teams have only a manager and a pitching coach, so a reserve player has to carry out that chore.

Savannah's designated hitter led off the frame with a single. Built like a fat beaver, Green had the land speed of that animal. Well aware of Green's deficiency in this area, Dews pointed to Bouton and ordered him to pinch run.

"I was really surprised when Bobby pointed at me to go in. Then I got psyched and was so excited that I almost fell down doing exercises to get loose," recalled Bouton.

The crowd of 884 came alive with Bouton's entrance into the contest. For Jim, it was the first time he had been on base since he played with the Houston Astros in 1970.

As he cautiously led off, it was obvious that he wasn't in familiar territory. Jim moved about the base paths as if they were a mine field.

Not much transpired from this maneuver. Bouton was erased on a force play at second base, although he did recall enough about this part of the game to execute a perfect slide into second.

After the game, Dews had some difficulty explaining why he pinch ran a 39-year-old for a 21-year-old prospect. "Well, we've had a lot of guys picked off lately. Jim ran the bases in the World Series and I figured, what the hell, it might wake us up," said Dews.

After their initial cold relations, Dews and Bouton grew closer as the season progressed. A *Sports Illustrated* article on the knuckleballer, appropriately titled "A Magnificent Obsession," seemed to seal their relationship. In that piece, writer Frank Deford did a section on Dews and all that this multitalented, intelligent man had given up for his love of the game. Reading of his own sacrifices made it easier for Dews to understand Bouton's motives.

Suddenly, Bouton wasn't quite so mysterious.

"The minor leagues were satisfying even when I couldn't win a game," Bouton was quoted as saying. "I've been happy for most of my life, but never more than now. Of course, the minors are not as good as the majors, but the question to me is whether the minors are better than the rest of life. And to me, they are."

Better than the rest of life, that's what baseball has always been to Bobby Dews. He could never understand how young prospects could say that they were going to give the game four or five years and then quit if they didn't make it. Dews would hear those words and think, "They just don't know what the rest of life is like."

Now Bobby Dews, age 39, knew what Jim Bouton, age 39, was after. He wanted to avoid the rest of life. And so did Dews. That's why he managed in the cow towns of Class A for nine years, why he takes delight in the mundane chores of throwing batting practice, hitting fungoes, and filling out lineup cards. All of that is so much better than the rest of life.

The article also pointed out that Bouton wasn't after more material for another book.

"Bouton's comeback has been so painfully extended that no one can any longer seriously suggest that he had been tramping through the bush leagues merely to research another book. One might as well say that Richard Nixon orchestrated Watergate merely to obtain anecdotal best seller material," pointed out Deford.

Reading this, Dews was convinced. And the sudden wave of publicity, being interviewed on television, on radio, and by the press, gratified his ego which had been walked on so many times in the ignobleness of Class A.

"You know, I've been quoted more in just this first half of the season than in my entire career altogether," said Dews. "I know it's because of Bouton. He's made the Savannah Braves the most widely known Class AA team around, and I'm probably the minor's most quoted manager. After all these years I'm really enjoying it."

The event which made Dews a Bouton fan occurred when Savannah was enroute to a 17–1 thrashing by Knoxville. The Braves had almost run through their pitching staff. Bouton had pitched two days before.

"I asked Jim if he would mind relieving and he said that he didn't want to. I thought he was being selfish and just worried about his ERA. The next inning he came up to me and said he was ready if I needed him. I still respect him for that," said Dews.

Bouton also became a Dews booster that night. On the bus trip following the rout, Dews didn't harangue his team as most mentors would; rather, he bought them two cases of beer and told them to forget about it.

Dews was a Bouton backer. While being careful not to go overboard in his praise of his older pitcher (for fear of looking foolish if Bouton made it to the majors and flopped), Bobby looked out for him. He was patient with Bouton and the quirks of the knuckleball. He treated Jim like any other prized prospect.

"There were times when I could've left Jim out there to get slaughtered, especially early in the season. But my job is to do what's right and that's what I tried to do with Bouton," said Dews.

One night when the knuckler was floating to the plate like a pitch in a Sunday picnic softball game, Atlanta Minor League Batting Instructor Luke Appling was overheard telling Dews to "leave that S.O.B. in there until he gives up 20 runs." Seventy-one-year-old Appling, a member of Baseball's Hall of Fame, thought Bouton should be placed in solitary confinement for life because of the disservice he did to the sport in *Ball Four*.

During his first month as a SavBrave, Jim tested Dews' patience; he had more ups and downs than a ferris wheel. After 61 innings he had allowed ten homers.

"All of this is incredibly frustrating," Bouton said. "I've

had a good knuckler but every time it doesn't break, they seem to hit it out."

The Grayson Stadium left-field porch was taking its toll. He was drilled for three home runs by Knoxville, which dropped his record to 4–5 with a 3.68 ERA. Word came from Atlanta Minor League Director Hank Aaron, "Take Bouton out of the starting rotation."

Dews informed the former author of the decision and Bouton was furious. He immediately called his guardian angel, Ted Turner.

"Ted, this is Jim Bouton. I've got a problem."

"What's up?" asked Turner.

"They took me out of the rotation. They've put me in the bullpen as a long relief man on a team with the best pitching staff in the league. All the starters go at least seven innings."

"No kidding," said Turner. "Bill Lucas told me that you'd get plenty of work."

"I don't think so. I think they'd like to bury me in the bullpen. I'm happy with Savannah as long as I'm pitching. If I can't start here, loan me out to another team that needs a starter."

"Damn it, I want you pitching," said Turner. "I'm gonna call Lucas now and take care of this."

The edict traveled from Turner to Lucas to Aaron to Dews that Ted wanted Bouton starting. Since Ted owns the team, he gets what he wants. Dews had already told the press of the change in Jim's status. To protect himself, he made a practice of starting Bouton only in the second games of a series of doubleheaders which cropped up on the schedule, saying he needed an extra starter and Jim filled the role.

This deception didn't work because Bouton told the local press of his conversation with Turner. He seemed to enjoy the fact that he could call the club's owner on the phone and receive action. The whole affair just proved that Bouton was no ordinary bush leaguer.

Jim had been granted a temporary reprieve. He would have a few more starts. And then? Then those making the decisions would rule. Once again, it was stomach time. He didn't just have to pitch well, he had to win. Right in the middle of his midlife crisis was a new problem, the age-old question of how to get the batter out.

Somewhere in his guts, Jim Bouton found the answer. It's said that a knuckleball is destiny's child. Even a connoisseur of the pitch has no idea if it will move or not. It either does or it doesn't.

Well, Jim Bouton willed his pitch to move. It darted, it hopped, it sank, and it floated like a paper airplane in a hurricane. Suddenly, Jim had reeled off five straight wins. His record was 9–5, one of the best in the Southern League.

"I'm as ready as I'm going to be for the majors," Bouton was saying.

He was also passing out praise. Dews received quite a bit. Jim called him "one of the best managers you'll find." Another who received compliments was Stu Livingstone.

13

A New Roomate

Stu Livingstone, the man who considered Bouton an "old S.O.B.," the one who told Roger Alexander that he'd be sorry about choosing Jim as a roommate, took Alexander's place in Bouton's room when Roger was called up to Richmond.

"We used to talk a lot in the bullpen. He really knew baseball. I mean, he thought about things that the rest of us didn't pay any attention to," said Livingstone.

Livingstone and Jim found some common ground. They were both free agents and on the brash side. More than anything else, they agreed that the best thing about baseball was the pressure.

"I liked the idea Jim had about crucial games. He said you should make a game of pressure. Just keep thinking to yourself, 'Isn't this fun just to be out here when it really matters?' As a relief pitcher, this philosophy especially appealed to me.

"We got to be pretty close and when Roger left I decided to room with Jim because he's an interesting guy. Also, he ate health foods and I was a little overweight and needed to eat the right things. I figured that I'd start eating that stuff too if I moved in with him," said Livingstone.

At the time of their joining forces on the road, Livingstone was struggling. In that Knoxville game where Bouton won Dews' respect by agreeing to work in relief, Stu pitched two-thirds of an inning and was shelled for seven runs. He was 2–2 with a 3.86 ERA and worried that news of his release would be arriving any day.

As a helper, Bouton was even more effective with Livingstone than he had been with Alexander. Once again, the topic of discussion between Jim and his roommate was self-confidence and pitching with your stomach. "Pitching with your stomach is throwing a slider low, outside, and at the knees with the bases loaded and two strikes on the batter," Bouton would say. "It's knowing in your heart that you can throw that kind of pitch and then doing it."

A jocular, 6-foot-2, 185-pounder from Los Angeles, Stu had known about the powers of the stomach. It had carried him this far. It was his secret weapon, too.

The son of a Scottish soccer player who had played in the World Cup finals, Livingstone was going to be a professional athlete even if it destroyed him. A competitive nature was his calling card and as a youngster he would often berate his teammates for their mistakes. In other words, he had the same dreams and tools as young Jim Bouton.

By straining his body to its limit, Stu discovered that he could throw a baseball faster than any of his teammates. So he threw and threw, thinking only of speed. It is the fireballs who impress the big league scouts. But the harder Livingstone threw, the wilder he became.

For this reason, he was never drafted during his career. His speed made him a star prepster in Los Angeles, but the best he could do was receive a partial scholarship from Loyola of Los Angeles.

In college, he wanted to be better than the best college pitcher in the country. If he couldn't be the best, he could at least throw the hardest. Scouts would watch him play, make notes about the fact that he was faster than most prospects, but his wildness scared them even more than it did the opposing batters. His senior year was a typical Livingstone season, a 7–7 record and a 5.50 ERA with a high strikeout total and an even higher number of walks.

Four years had slipped by in what seemed like a quick doubleheader for Stu. The baseball draft came and went like the afternoon smog in Los Angeles, and his telephone never rang with the news he had been hoping for. He was 21 years old and through. A has-been. A guy with a decent fast ball who never developed, according to the scouts.

It was summer in Southern California and Stu Livingstone couldn't believe that his seasons in the sun on the diamond were over. Calling every scout who had ever watched him throw, Livingstone ran up a $100 phone bill and found no one even willing to take a second look.

Finally, he heard of a tryout camp being held by baseball's Central Scouting Bureau, a talent finding organization backed by most of the major league clubs who share its reports.

He stood among 300 hopefuls clad in gas station shirts, sandals, jeans, and tennis hats. Livingstone looked around him and saw that his professional dreams had come down to trying out with a bunch of guys who should have been playing softball.

The scouts asked him to throw one pitch. He did and was invited back to the next day's session. He pitched for ten minutes the following day and was told that a team would contact him.

Weeks passed and once again there was no word. Stu was working for his father at an oil refinery. His job was digging ditches. One day the temperature was 104 degrees and he felt as though he was burying his dreams with every shovel full of dirt.

Then Atlanta scout Tom Morgan called Livingstone. They set up a meeting in the parking lot of Loyola of Los Angeles, where he would try to impress Morgan.

The scout had on a catcher's mitt and Stu began throwing like a robot at high speed. Morgan convinced Stu that there was more to pitching than trying to throw a ball at the speed of sound. In short, Morgan taught him about control, showed him a slider and a sinker, and slowed him down. He also had a contract in his hand.

Livingstone went to Bradenton in the rookie Gulf Coast League. Following Morgan's advice, he had a 3–5 record with a 1.67 ERA and a no-hitter. In 1976 he was switched to the bullpen, performed admirably, and moved up the minor league ladder.

He still thinks back to those days of digging ditches in 100 degree heat. Despite pitching well, he worries that his release could come at any time. He is now 23 and the Braves have invested little in him. A few bad outings could make him expendable.

If it were all to end now, Livingstone wouldn't be the same downtrodden athlete he was right after college. Every year at Loyola's alumni baseball game he sees his collegiate teammates, who never had a chance to turn pro. For the most part, they are bitter. They won't even attend baseball games any more, but train hard for a month before the alumni contest. They long to show that someone, somewhere has made a mistake about them. Livingstone says that if it weren't for that last tryout camp, he probably would be the same way.

By the end of the 1978 season it was apparent that it would still be some time before Livingstone was relegated to competing only in the college alumni games. Rather, he had established himself as a major league prospect with a 7–4 record, a 2.88 ERA, and six saves.

Stu will say that rooming with Bouton made a big difference. His mental approach changed: he became more positive and his confidence was renewed. During the span he stayed with the knuckleballer, he had a 1.32 ERA and a string of 28 scoreless innings (just two short of a Southern League record).

"It's nice to know that I helped Stu," recalled Bouton. "But he really made a difference with me. He helped me develop my slider and sinker."

When Bouton was slogging through his mediocre performances, he and Livingstone came to a conclusion. "I needed more than just a knuckleball to make it back," said Bouton. "The knuckler was fine and I still had the palm ball from my Yankee days, but I needed more," said Bouton.

Johnny Sain had worked with Jim on a slider and sinker and he employed them occasionally, but he lacked the confidence to use them often. The slider and sinker are Livingstone's staples. Every day Bouton and Stu would head to the bullpen to work on these new weapons.

After one game in which Bouton had thrown the two new pitches effectively, he told the press, "I'm going to have to take Stu with me when I make it up. He's a great coach."

Their relationship flowered and Livingstone loved to be quoted about Bouton. He, more than anyone else, had clear insights into the former television reporter's stay in Savannah. "The players accepted him, but he still was different from the rest of us. He was at least fifteen years older than anyone else, along with being a TV star, an author, and more intelligent, and he had won 20 games in the Big Show and in a couple World Series. That always set him apart in the minors."

These differences were illustrated when Jim would go out with his SavBrave friends. "Every once in a while I would be brought up short," recalled Bouton. "I'd be in a place with a table full of guys and the conversation would be interesting, when in would walk a couple of 19-year-olds and the guys would point and yell at them. They were barely out of high school, these girls. Almost children. I wasn't interested."

One evening an old lady with blue hair walked into a bar. Bouton's teammates teased, "There's your date, Jim." "Hell, I'm not ready for blue hair yet." said Jim.

According to Livingstone, they didn't engage in the girl-chasing, peeping Tom activities Bouton described in *Ball Four*.

"Jim liked to read a lot and he'd fix meals in the room. We'd go out and have a few drinks, but we didn't go after women. Actually, I think we both feel sex is great, but pitching is even better. Baseball dominated our conversations. Now and then he started talking about his personal problems, but I didn't want to hear that stuff and he knew it."

There was one disadvantage to having Jim Bouton as a roommate: the media. Bouton was, in essence, a politician when it came to those in the news business.

"The phone was always ringing. He was always on it, talking to some guy from Philadelphia or somewhere. He really loves the publicity and doesn't just cooperate, he goes out of his way to encourage it. It was like he was running for public office and he had to win everybody over to his side. He wanted people to like him and respect what he was doing.

"Another thing about Jim's relationship with the media was his brashness. If you asked him an innocent question like how he was doing, he'd say 'I have one one-hitter, two two-hitters,' and so on. He liked the limelight, and the rest of the guys on the team didn't resent it. They never had had the publicity and Jim wasn't like some former major leaguers who talked about the old days with the Yankees," explained Livingstone.

Stu also appreciated Bouton's physical attributes. "Genetically, he's an amazing athlete. While it's true that he really works hard and eats the right things, there's something in his makeup that make his knees hold together. He's not imposing physically, but he's strong. He made 21 starts in the worst league in the country where it's hot as hell every day. He was going strong at the end when everybody else was tired. It was amazing."

Livingstone has no regrets about rooming with Bouton.

"The experience was super. I mean, it was the greatest summer of my life. Besides, it gives me something to talk about. People ask me all the time what Bouton is really like. They all think he's weird. Hell, there were four or five guys with Savannah who were a lot crazier than he is. Those guys were nuts; I guess you could just say that Jim is eccentric," concluded Livingstone.

14

The Clubhouse Lawyer

"I was a hard worker, a good battler. I fielded my position well, but the word on me is that I'm a clubhouse lawyer."

This was the way Jim Bouton thought the baseball world felt about him at the time he wrote *Ball Four*. Eight years later with the Savannah Braves, this description still applied.

Actually, Bouton worked on "being one of the boys" with Savannah, and for the most part, he succeeded. His age and experience set him apart, but with these minor leaguers (many of whom had read *Ball Four* in their impressionable teenage years) Jim was more comfortable than he ever was during his first trek in the majors.

Bouton spent his days on the road in the same places as these fellows who were struggling on $900 a month (Bouton made $1,000) and $7.50 per day meal money. The lack of funds meant that there were few luxurious trips on the town. They spent their days wandering through shopping malls, looking at the paperbacks in the drug stores and the newest fashions in store windows.

It was a chain restaurant and motel existence. Their rooms were in Days Inns and Holiday Inns, the same ones that accommodate typical traveling salesmen. They stayed at clean places with a color television in working order to keep them entertained. When not watching the tube or hanging around stores, they ate at Waffle Houses and Sambos, the places that were open 24 hours and could serve a hungry team inexpensively after an 8 P.M. game.

What these players had was plenty of spare time and they filled those hours talking. They complained about their status, the pains and depressions of the bushes, and Jim Bouton listened. He made their troubles his own, sympathized with them and offered his views.

Jim was careful not to be overbearing about his feelings toward the sport's establishment. He was still convinced that baseball was run by a bunch of money-grubbing monarchs with Neanderthal mentalities and elephant memories when it came to recalling those who had sinned against the grand old game. Nonetheless, he did his best to follow the party line and keep his critics silent.

When a pair of Savannah players abandoned the team at midseason, walking out despite being in the starting lineup, Bouton's comments on the situation made every baseball conservative smile. Seldom do players leave of their own accord at midseason. In his eight years of managing, Bobby Dews had seen only one of the over 250 athletes he managed retire this way.

"Most athletes who quit don't realize the seriousness of their actions until later," said Bouton. "One day they'll be at home and it will suddenly strike them. They'll miss it, and they'll meet doctors, lawyers, and other professional people who'd give almost anything for a chance to play pro ball. They'll wonder why they quit. Today's athletes are used to being coddled and having everything taken care of for them. They're special people and treated that way. These guys today just don't have the stick-to-itiveness of those when I first came up. They want immediate gratification and if they don't get it, they quit and go to work in Dad's bank."

Bouton was doing his best to shed the "clubhouse lawyer" label, but that didn't stop players from asking for his advice.

One athlete who approached Bouton was Lelan Byrd.

In essence, baseball had turned Lelan Byrd into nothing more than a piece of equipment that disappeared from the field when the game began. Every team has a guy like Byrd. He's a spare part that's never needed. His purpose is to take up space and help the manager with things like infield and batting practice. In the minors, this role used to be filled by an older player who was happy just to be part of the game and collect a paycheck, an athlete who was void of hopes and dreams.

But Lelan wasn't some broken veteran en route to becoming a bush league manager. At 22, he still felt he was a valuable commodity, the player to whom the Atlanta Braves had given a $15,000 bonus at age 18. But a broken hand, along with ankle and serious knee injuries, tainted his value in the view of the front office. All of this made Byrd, a genuinely good person who had a 3.7 grade point average in pre-medicine while attending college in the off-season, a perfect candidate to be that extra bolt which is nice to have around, to handle all the unpleasant chores that have to be done on the team, but is never needed to keep the machine operating.

The inactivity and the fear that any day a release was coming had Lelan scared. He and Bouton had lockers next to each other and they often discussed his situation. Lelan was an admirer of Jim and one of his staunchest defenders on the team.

Bouton thought Lelan "was a good kid who's getting screwed. It's just hard to ask a young kid with hopes to accept the fact that he isn't going anywhere. Every team needs someone like Lelan, but it's very difficult for the player to accept the fact that he's not a prospect."

Byrd's plight reached a crisis when the team completed a

114

three-game series in Atlanta playing right in front of the major league club. Before departing the Georgia capital, almost every player who was spending his first summer in Class AA received a $1,000 check from the Braves front office as his incentive bonus. An incentive bonus is written into every minor leaguer's contract. After spending 90 days in Class A, they receive $500. After 90 days in Class AA, there's a $1,000 reward. Byrd had idled the needed time away on the Savannah bench, batting only 21 times, and the front office had no check for him.

Byrd was twice put on the disabled list and those inactive days on the team didn't count toward the magic number of 90. Lelan was incensed by this, saying that he wasn't hurt when he was placed on the list and that he had agreed to fake an injury just to give the front office more time to alleviate some roster problems.

He took his troubles to Bouton, and if anyone ever needed a lawyer, it was Lelan Byrd. Bouton listened and offered advice which proved to be the ideal counsel.

He told Lelan to take his plight of never playing to the press. Meanwhile, Bouton told a local reporter of Byrd's difficulty over his incentive bonus and asked the scribe to call the front office and ask some questions.

It worked perfectly. Byrd told the reporter of his plight. "I feel like an ornament on a Christmas tree. I take infield practice, throw batting practice, warm up pitchers, but never play. They give everybody a chance but me. My teammates see what's happening and it's humiliating."

Bobby Dews pointed out that Lelan had hit over .200 just once in his four minor league years and that, while he had a fine glove, his range had been seriously hampered by a knee injury. Nevertheless, Dews began inserting Byrd into the lineup and he ended the year as Savannah's regular third baseman.

As for his incentive bonus, that never appeared in the paper. The front office told the press that Byrd would receive his money before the year ended, and he did.

To this day, Lelan Byrd is thankful to Bouton for his

advice. As for Jim Bouton, he was happy to help someone else out and not be criticized for it. The clubhouse lawyer was still in business, but he had mellowed.

15

The Last Bus Ride

There is no way to sleep on a bus. Oh, it is possible to doze for 20 to 30 minutes, but the sleep is that of the restless, aching kind, the type a bruised boxer experiences after a fight. The problem with sleeping on a bus is that there is always an armrest sticking in your back or the dilemma of what to do about your feet.

Bobby Dews, who has been riding minor league buses since he was eight years old and a bat boy for his father's teams, would sit erect in the first seat, his chin supported by his hand, staring straight out the front window through his glasses. As anyone who approached him discovered, Dews was asleep in this posture. But the rest wouldn't last long; he would waken every half hour, stand up and stretch, and then return to his original pose, closing his eyes.

On buses, Jim Bouton seldom slept. Usually he talked or

read books on such topics as Eastern religions and psychology.

This was August, the "dog days," as the players call the month. In the Southern League, the temperature and humidity rarely slipped below 90 as long as the sun was up. The bus trips became torture. After riding fourteen hours from Savannah to Memphis, the players felt as though they had been clobbered in several choice spots with a two-by-four. One emerged from these cross-country rides grimy, sweaty, and exhausted.

It was also the time manic depression captured the psyche of many an athlete. They had been playing almost every day for five months. By August, the batting and earned run averages were just about fixed. The tale of the season has been told and most players wanted just to go home and never ever ride a bus again. Men who have spent their lives in the minors swear off baseball for good this time of year, only to return in the spring.

As was the case with the rest of his teammates, Jim Bouton went through a mental slump during this month. Based on his performance with a glove on his left hand, one would never have guessed that Bouton was undergoing any type of trauma. He had reeled off five straight wins and was in the midst of his best streak since his last great season with the Yankees in 1964.

While other pitchers were asking to be lifted after seven innings, Bouton was going the distance. On one 96 degree August night in Savannah, he worked thirteen innings, winning a 2–1 decision with the only Nashville run coming in the first frame. He'd dash to the mound, sweat filling his hair, face, and uniform, making him appear as if he just stepped out of a shower. Like a stubborn Christian refusing to be eaten by the lions, he lasted the entire 3 hours and 17 minutes and stranded twelve Nashville runners.

It was an incredible accomplishment for any Southern League pitcher. For a 39-year-old to work thirteen innings, throw 165 pitches, and appear ready for more was almost a miracle, and Bouton knew it.

"I'm ready to pitch in Atlanta or anywhere else," Bouton said. "People just haven't hit the ball hard off me in the last month. I really believe that I deserve a major league shot. I've won and shown that age isn't a factor. I've pitched extra inning games and complete games after ten-hour bus rides. I threw a one-hitter after an all-night bus ride."

Then Bouton would recite the litany which became very familiar to those around him during the month of August. "I have one one-hitter, one two-hitter, two three-hitters . . ."

Salesman Jim Bouton was pushing harder than ever to market himself. His credentials were impressive, and by the end of the season he would have a 12–9 record with a 2.77 ERA and twelve complete games.

As he liked to point out, "It is one of the best records in the Braves' organization. When you consider the fact that I didn't start until May 23, I could have easily won fifteen or sixteen games. Also, I pitched for the cycle. I had one one-hitter, two two-hitters, three three-hitters, and four four-hitters."

Bouton was doing well, very well. And he wanted the world to know about it. He also was panicking.

The Atlanta Braves had suddenly come alive and were moving in on fifth place and a .500 record. This was bad news to Bouton, who knew that the worse the team performed, the sooner and more likely would be his promotion.

He began to worry. While other players thought of going home during those long, sticky August bus rides, Bouton pondered the possibility of his dream crumbling. Here he was pitching well, better than he had for fourteen years, and it just might not do any good. He felt like the proverbial donkey chasing the carrot and suddenly realizing that there was no reward at the journey's end.

"About the middle of August, Jim began to think that he wasn't going to pull it off. He talked about it a lot," said roommate Stu Livingstone.

Bouton swung into action. He wrote his guardian angel, the man who gave him the nod when all the others just shook their heads no.

Ted Turner received a two-page letter from Bouton along with a photostat page of quotes on Jim from various papers across the Southern League. In this letter which Bouton showed to several people including Livingstone, Jim praised Turner's imagination, saying that only someone like Ted would have the intelligence and guts to give Bouton a chance. Bouton also proclaimed that "for the first time, I'm ready to pitch in the majors. Just as he "willed" his way back into baseball, he was doing the same thing in his trek back to the Big Leagues.

"I know that I'll disturb the clubhouse when I arrive and I don't want to do that when the club is doing so well," continued the letter. "So I'm willing to finish the season here and help Bobby Dews in the Southern League pennant race. Then I can join the team in September."

The letter also stated that Bouton "was willing to sign a blank contract over the winter. You [Turner] fill in the figures. Money isn't important because I'll make millions in the off-season."

Bouton again praised Turner's imagination at the end of the letter and used the pronoun "we" when talking about his future plans with the Braves.

He mailed it to the Braves' owner care of TV-17, Turner's cable television, to make sure it was not intercepted by the Braves' other executives. The text, along with the newspaper clippings, illustrated Bouton's good attitude and his hustle, characterizing him as a "clean liver." It was a perfect package for a man who was appealing to the mind of an advertising tycoon.

The knuckleball pitcher was also continually making his case in the media. He would welcome reporters with such glee and enthusiasm that he was willing to supply them with everything just short of a pen and notebook.

This was graphically demonstrated when David Marash and ABC's "20/20" news crew arrived in Savannah to film a documentary on the team's celebrity. A camera followed Bouton everywhere on and off the field. He ran extra sprints for the project, agreed to wear a wireless microphone while pitching, and gave the TV people complete access to the field. Bouton was filmed from directly behind the catcher, from deep center field, and from the dugout.

Said Dews later: "It's the middle of a close game and I'm trying to figure out who to pinch hit. I look over my shoulder and there's this woman, a TV person, wearing a long skirt sitting next to me. I couldn't believe she was there in the middle of a game."

"Towards the end, the TV people really got to be a pain in the butt," recalled Savannah relief pitcher Tim Graven. "Those people from '20/20' turning on those hot, bright lights really got to most of us. It was hot, the 'dog days,' and these people just really seemed in the way. It put everybody on edge."

In defense of Bouton, it must be pointed out that he always cleared his media endeavors with the Savannah manager first. Dews, an easy man to get along with, usually just approved the schemes, not being familiar with the ways of television after spending his life in the low minors.

As was true of his entire career, Bouton was better than ever when the "20/20" television lights were turned on. He was pitching with just two days rest and fired a three-hit shutout over Columbus. For dramatic effect Jim fanned the side in the final inning.

"I was more nervous with the '20/20' people here than ever before with television," said Bouton. "I'm not really sure why that was; I just knew that I had to do well."

What Bouton wasn't saying was that Turner would hear about the "20/20" game and watch it the following week. A good performance would bring added pressure on the Atlanta owner. Also, Jim was the "Bulldog" and he wanted to show his guts and determination when it meant the most.

Another reason he longed to do well on television was that he thought Turner wasn't being told about his success. Jim felt that General Manager Bill Lucas and Minor League Director Hank Aaron didn't want Turner to know of his deeds. This was the reason Bouton mailed his letter to Ted care of his television station and it's also why he presented his merits on a public forum.

"It's low-hit games that I win which Turner hears about. If I pitch well but lose, he doesn't know because word doesn't get out," Bouton said on a few occasions.

When dealing with the front office, Jim always displayed more than a trace of paranoia. He believed that baseball's establishment viewed him only as "the guy who wrote that book." He felt that they thought of him as a traitor and a prodigal son who they never wanted to see again.

There was also more than a tinge of guilt in Jim's relationship with the sport's brass. Publicly, he'll never admit to anything being wrong or unethical about *Ball Four*, but down deep, in the back of his psyche, doubts linger. This was another source of his uneasiness and latent guilt feelings. But, as the saying goes, even paranoids have enemies. So does Bouton.

Atlanta Manager Bobby Cox is one.

A former Yankee coach who labored long and played with Bouton in the New York organization, Cox still views him as a clubhouse lawyer who shattered the Yankee mystique with his book. While he and Bouton had played together, they didn't know each other very well. But Cox, a military-looking man with the short hair of a junior officer, had the line on him from old Yankee friends and the word wasn't very complimentary.

On the Braves' coaching staff are three other ex-Yankees: Cloyd Boyer, Pete Ward, and Clete Boyer. After *Ball Four*, Clete Boyer and Bouton hadn't spoken to each other. Even before the book, Bouton's brashness and opinionated personality galled Clete. The book only reaffirmed his impression of Jim.

Hank Aaron is another who considers Bouton "a problem." He felt humiliated when Ted Turner overruled the release of Bouton in the spring. In his first season as Minor League Director, Aaron didn't enjoy having his authority questioned by Bouton's existence. Aaron sought to prove that he wasn't just a figurehead, that he was more than part of the furniture in the Atlanta front office. Also, a man who felt he was never fully appreciated by the fans, despite his breaking the legendary Babe Ruth's home run record, Aaron couldn't understand all the excitement over a 39-year-old pitcher with a 62–61 lifetime major league record.

Bouton feels that Aaron's animosity toward him goes back to 1970. Jim, Aaron, and Willie Mays were appearing on the Dick Cavett Show to discuss *Ball Four*. Cavett asked Aaron what he thought of the book and Hank followed the baseball establishment's lead and discussed it with the same contempt with which Joseph McCarthy spoke of the *Communist Manifesto*. Mays did the same.

In rebuttal, Bouton asked if either of the great athletes had read the book. As was usually the case with *Ball Four* critics, neither had, and both admitted it. Cavett then ignored the two superstars for the remaining hour and talked to Bouton about his book. Naturally, Aaron and Mays were embarrassed, and Bouton believes that this was the beginning of his trouble with Aaron.

Like almost everyone else in the Braves system, Jim considered the Braves General Manager Bill Lucas a fair man, but he was far from being an open Bouton supporter like Turner. Bouton continually worried that Cox and Aaron had convinced Lucas and Turner that they should bury their minor league knuckleball pitcher.

The pressure on the Atlanta front office was mounting. *The Atlanta Constitution* had run several features on Bouton throughout the summer and followed his progress closely. Almost daily, some reporter would ask Lucas and Aaron, "When is Bouton coming to Atlanta?"

Bouton was also queried on the subject of his return to the majors. His situation was similar to that of a man awaiting the governor's reprieve before facing an execution; Jim's future hung on the words of those above him. Finally, the not knowing was just too much for him to handle. Like the condemned man, Bouton tried to force a decision, using his only weapon—his mouth.

"If baseball doesn't give me a chance now after I've pitched this well, then it's obvious that they just don't want me," Bouton told *The Atlanta Constitution*. "They've got to give me a chance. I've earned it and the fans want to see me get a shot. I've spent two years in the minors and won more games in Class AA than many major league pitchers. I'm no gimmick. They say my knuckleball isn't as good as Phil Niekro's. That's like comparing everybody's fast ball to Tom Seaver's. Mine's good enough and that's all that matters.

"Baseball people have always said they like the way I perform in the clutch and how I am a hard worker with a lot of desire. But none of that seems to matter because some people just look at me as the guy who wrote that book. If the Braves and Ted Turner don't give me a chance in view of their pitching, who will?" explained Bouton.

Jim also was overly concerned about what the Atlanta coaching staff's reaction to him would be. He was convinced that his hustling style would win over Cox, "But what's Cloyd Boyer going to think when I'm praising Johnny Sain, the man right below him in the minors? Boyer can't help a pitcher like Sain can."

Another of Bouton's favorite activities was speculating about the conversations that were going on about him in the Atlanta front office. "They're trying to figure out if I'm a prospect. Some are saying I'm too old. But I was 39 when I signed and I'm still 39. They couldn't have expected me to get any younger and I haven't aged rapidly during the summer. If I wasn't a prospect, why did they sign me in the first place?" Bouton would ask with a smile.

There is no question that Bouton was the center of some interesting discussions in the Braves' front office. Most of the team's executives didn't think the knuckleballer would put them in this situation. They had hoped that Bouton would start a few games, get hit hard, and be quietly released, as had been the case in Knoxville and Durango the year before. Thus, Ted Turner would be placated.

Atlanta's pitching was dreadful. The staff's ERA was hovering at the 4.20 mark and only Phil Niekro, rookie Larry

McWilliams, and reliever Gene Garber kept them above AAA level. By the end of August, the Braves had sunk to the bottom faster than an anchor. Attendance was nonexistent. There were some crowds (which were more like gatherings of a few masochists) in the 1,500 range.

September 1, the day when major league baseball teams expand their rosters from 25 to 40 players, came and went. No announcement about Bouton was made because the Savannah Braves had miraculously made the playoffs.

Savannah had gone through 38 players and the Grayson Stadium clubhouse seemed more like a bus station than anything else because someone was always coming or going with his arms full of luggage. Injuries in Atlanta, plus a certain lack of organization by the front office, caused this constant shifting of personnel. Bobby Dews' team went through seven third basemen, six keystone combinations, and five catchers. Some athletes were forced to fill in at positions they had never played before.

Nonetheless, the end of the season came and Savannah had won the Southern League's Eastern Division second half championship by a mere four percentage points over Jacksonville. Like Job, Dews had suffered and survived more setbacks than seemed humanly possible, and he was honored as the loop's manager of the year. Bouton also received an award. He was picked as the league's "Top Hustler" because of his enthusiasm, diving plays in the field, and determination. Hearing of the award, Savannah's General Manager Dave Fendrick said, "Bouton is a hustler all right. In two years everyone from Ted Turner on down will see how Bouton hustled us all."

Winning the division meant quite a bit to Jim. He put the team's struggle against adversity in the same class as his almost impossible comeback. "We were like a group of guys climbing Mt. Everest and the people on top were throwing rocks and oil down on us," said Bouton, who also used the identical metaphor to characterize his quest.

The SavBraves were to face Orlando, the first half division winner, in a short playoff series. If they won, they would then play Knoxville in a best of three-game set to determine the Southern League Champion. Knoxville had won both halves and so was the Western Division champion of the Southern League.

Savannah lost the first game in Orlando and the series switched to Grayson Stadium with Bouton on the mound.

This was to be the final chapter of his fairy tale summer in Savannah and Bouton knew it. He desperately wanted to put an exclamation point after what he calls "the greatest summer of my life." There was no better spot for the "Bulldog" to do just that than in a crucial situation in the playoffs.

In this, the summer of his life, the season when time stood still and then took a few paces backward for Jim, he came up with one last great game. Having characterized his return to the diamond as "David trying to beat Goliath without a slingshot," Bouton needed only a knuckleball. He had the "superknuck," as he calls the pitch which moves up and down, left and right. He lobbed a two-hitter, beating Orlando 4–1.

After the game, Bouton began his litany. "I've now pitched for the cycle. I have one one-hitter, two two-hitters, three three-hitters . . ."

The press interrupted his chant with the notice that it was no longer necessary. Hank Aaron had arrived in the second inning of the game and left in the eighth accompanied by a guard supplied by the city. Before departing, Aaron said that, "Bouton will get his chance in Atlanta at the end of the playoffs."

It was over. Once again, David had triumphed.

Bouton refused to comment on the news. He hadn't been told officially, but he knew that this was the word he had been longing for.

By coming late and leaving early, Aaron had avoided stopping in the clubhouse to talk with Bouton, Dews, or anyone else. This was to be the Atlanta Minor League Director's one and only trip to Grayson Stadium for a SavBrave game in 1978. The Savannah management and players felt that

126

Aaron had purposely ignored them all year and they didn't enjoy toiling in complete anonymity.

Savannah won the third game with Orlando and then moved into the Southern League finals against Knoxville. Nothing more about the Bouton situation had been said. Thursday, prior to the opening contest with Knoxville at Grayson, Jim Bouton walked into Dews' office. The knuckleball pitcher began thanking his mentor for the pleasant summer. He repeated what he had often said publicly about Dews, calling him one of the best managers he had ever played under. Bouton added that he would always remember and cherish his relationship with Bobby.

Throughout the conversation, Bobby Dews was befuddled. Then it finally dawned on him: Bouton was leaving the team and going to Atlanta right in the middle of the playoffs.

As it turned out, Bouton had received a telephone call from Bill Lucas telling him that he was to report to the team Friday and that he would pitch Sunday against the Dodgers. No one in the Atlanta front office had had the courtesy to give Dews the message that his best pitcher would soon be leaving. This was indicative of the manner in which the Braves treated Dews during the entire season.

"You would think that someone up there would think I was doing a good job. I think I do well, but I never hear anything. That's the way baseball works, but at times it's hard to swallow," Dews said during one of the many communication miscues between Atlanta and Savannah.

The Bouton call-up in the middle of the playoffs was greeted with anger and dismay by the Savannah fans. They had viewed the parade of new faces all summer as an act of contempt by the Braves' front office. They had taken to Bouton's style of play and willingness to mingle with the people in the stands. He had become the biggest hero to hit the town in a long, long time. Now he was whisked away when the team needed him most.

In Atlanta Bouton was giving interviews and talking about pitching against the Dodgers. Meanwhile, Savannah lost the playoffs to Knoxville. In the final contest of the playoffs, a game which Bouton was supposed to have pitched, Savannah was clobbered 9–1.

Had he pitched in the finals, Bouton might have been drubbed, but the Savannah fans wouldn't accept that idea. Bouton had become an idol, winning almost every clutch contest he worked. The fans felt he could have brought the town its first league championship since 1940.

To this day, Bobby Dews is convinced Bouton would have won that final playoff game for his team. "When Bouton was called up, it took something out of the team. He had won so many crucial games for us. I know that the Braves needed him as a drawing card, but all we needed him for was one more game. To me, it was the most important game of my life and I would have liked him out there," concluded Dews.

16

The Family

The scene was domestic. A large black dog barked at the screen door, but as soon as the guests entered he started licking hands and wagging his tail. Jim Bouton sat on a large screened porch with a view of the beach and ocean, and he talked as the family began to wander through. It was late August, and the season was almost over.

As he spoke, Bobbie Bouton, his wife, arrived on the porch. She was carrying a large cardboard box, packing things in preparation for their departure. The lease on the beach home ended September 1, and the family didn't know where it would be after that date. No word had come from Atlanta on whether the pitcher would be promoted by the big league club when the Southern League season was over September 4.

If Bouton did get the call, he wanted his family with him in Atlanta, and they would follow him to the Georgia capital.

If the good news didn't come, the family would return home to Englewood, New Jersey.

In the meantime, with the lease over and nowhere to go for four days, Bobbie was making phone calls and arranging to stay with relatives in Beaufort, South Carolina, some 30 miles away. The boxes she was packing were to be mailed back to New Jersey. She drives an old station wagon, and Bobbie did not want it completely overloaded on their trip to wherever.

For many women, the uncertainty, the moves, the life of being a baseball player's wife is difficult to take, but Bobbie Bouton seemed to thrive on it. In the last two seasons she had to move the family to Knoxville, Durango, Portland, and now Savannah, but there were no complaints. She will tell anyone, "I always liked being a baseball wife best."

Part of being a baseball wife is packing, and she continued to do that as her husband sat and talked to an interviewer. Occasionally, she would add a point or two.

It was late morning, and the three children, who had apparently arisen only shortly before, wandered through the porch. They were bright, attractive, and alert, and they were completely comfortable with someone interviewing their father. They have seen much of it during the summer in Savannah. At times, they would interrupt or tell their father to recount a certain story. He feigned anger and asked them who was giving the interview, but he did not really object.

A local TV reporter arrived with a camera and began shooting scenes of the life of the Boutons at home. The children acted naturally with the camera running. The oldest, Michael, age 14, even volunteered scenes he thought would be appropriate for the cameraman, and he dragged the somewhat bemused reporter to the kitchen to film the health foods in the refrigerator. They came out shortly, saying there was not enough light in the kitchen. Michael let it be known that this was probably a good thing, because there were still dirty dishes in the sink. An accusing finger was pointed at David Bouton.

Bobbie, who was carrying one of the boxes, smiled.

130

"There's been too much swearing in this house lately," she explained. A penalty had been instituted and the last one caught cursing was responsible for the next meal's dishes.

David had been the latest victim for a rule that obviously did not include the father. David sat off to one side, and he grinned, enjoying the whole commotion. He is the Korean war orphan the Boutons adopted during the writing of *Ball Four*. He is 13 and has a surprising facial resemblance to his adoptive father. He seemed to be getting a kick out of the activities of his hyper siblings but did not relish the spotlight as they did.

The youngest, Laurie, age 11, was rushing all over the room. The phone rang and she answered it quickly and began an animated conversation. She put her hand over the phone and said a name, asking her mother who it was. Bobbie replied that it was the ex-trainer for the Portland Mavericks. Laurie said she still didn't remember but continued talking until her father pulled the phone away and took the call from his old friend.

The TV cameraman was still recording the family, and the reporter asked Bouton a few questions as Laurie went over to her mother and sat in her lap. The camera swung her way and she jumped. "Don't film me sitting in her lap," and she headed to a chair, where she assumed a more grown-up position. A few minutes later the cameraman took them out on the beach and down to the water slide where he could film the family man, Jim Bouton, with his children.

The location is Tybee Island, Georgia. It had been known as Savannah Beach until four months before, when the local residents decided they needed a name and image change. It still remains a fairly run-down, residential beach, seventeen miles from Savannah, primarily a commuting resort for the area residents. On Bouton's initial arrival in Savannah, he took a small motel room at the beach, and when his family arrived at the end of the school term, they were able to secure an economical rental agreement on an ocean-front house. With the beach and the area's historical sights, it was a good summer for the family.

Bouton's children have learned to take the moves in stride, and Bouton feels that this experience was good for them.

"Ideally, if you could program this kind of controlled crisis into a kid's life, you would. I think it is going to be better for them that they have seen their old man struggling," Bouton said. The uncertainty does not give any outward appearance of disrupting the children's personalities.

"When all the kids at school learned that Dad was going back to baseball," recalled Michael, "they called him an old man and said he'd never make it. They said he was stupid to leave television where he was a star."

Michael Bouton idolizes his father. As demonstrated by his actions with the television reporter, he sort of views himself as his dad's press agent. "I'd just tell the kids that my dad was doing what he wants. He was being happy," added Michael, who has learned the family line quite well.

Michael then brought out a shark fin and said that he likes swimming with it under water and scaring people. "I've got a lot of practical jokes. The shark fin is one of the best. It's almost as good a joke as the one Dad pulled on Don Collins," added Michael.

While Dad may be improving his psyche riding life out in the bushes, it hasn't been easy for the kids.

"Actually, this is the first time I remember my dad having a good record. All the other times he was sort of lousy, I mean mediocre," said Michael, who couldn't wait to return to school and boast of Jim's successes.

Later in the season, when Bouton made his debut in Atlanta, Michael spelled out the word "JIM" in the center-field grandstand by pushing down the seats. It was the statement of a son who had struggled with his father's actions and worried over his future. It turned out that Bouton was right and the world was going to know it with Michael passing the word.

It is Bobbie Bouton who runs the household and keeps the children in line. "It's a big responsibility. The kids know that I'm not very good at discipline. They take advantage of me," said Bobbie.

For a time, the family adopted a "Wait until your father gets home!" approach to reprimanding the children. "But I wasn't very good at that," admitted Jim. "When I got home I felt more like playing with them than yelling at them."

So it's Bobbie who makes the rules. Jim is like an older brother to the children. They'll go to him for advice, but he just doesn't seem like a father. At 39, he really doesn't seem like a minor leaguer either.

Jim and Bobbie Bouton met when the knuckleballer was a freshman at Western Michigan University. "All Bobbie liked to talk about was baseball. She was the scorekeeper for her high school team and Al Kaline and the Detroit Tigers were her heroes," recalled Jim.

In fact, Bobbie thought that the only reason her new boyfriend went out for the freshman baseball team was to impress her. She changed her mind about that one day when she saw him throwing in the gym. Bobbie predicted a major league career for Jim and to this day Bouton refers to his wife as "a great scout."

Since then, she has followed as Jim's personality continued to leapfrog. "I've been reading this book, *Changes*, and it's about the different stages we all go through. Sometimes I worry that I'm not keeping up with him," said Bobbie.

She sees a quest for lost youth as part of Jim's trek back to baseball. "The last few years he's been very concerned about his looks. He works out almost every night in the off-season, has more cooking utensils than anything else to take care of his health food, and he likes being around young people."

Jim Bouton was looking for the fountain of youth in the bushes, and his family was there. It wasn't easy, as a friend of the family explained to *The Atlanta Journal*. "He [Bouton] disregarded his family entirely. The needs were purely selfish. That's probably a healthy thing, but it's all one way. Jim sold the house and lost a couple of years of income. By his own figures, this probably cost him $250,000. There's no ulterior motive here. He's doing it to do it."

One writer said that, "Life with Jim Bouton has just the right amount of insecurity to make it interesting."

Lately, his life has been more like a roller coaster ride. It's fun for a time, but eventually people want to get off. Bobbie Bouton had a front seat on the roller coaster. She tried to comprehend what kept her husband running.

"I really do understand why he had to go play ball again. He had been talking about it for a long time, and after the TV series failed, he needed it as a kind of therapy. After he came back, I really knew that he could make it. I saw him improve and for a time it seemed like he and I were the only ones who thought so."

There was even some dissension within the Bouton clan about Jim's likelihood of success. Bobbie and David Bouton had a $5 bet, with Bobbie taking the position that her husband would return to the majors. Then again, what else would one expect from Jim Bouton's cheerleader?

"Being a baseball wife isn't as bad as some people think. I like traveling and we've been able to do a lot of it because Jim's in the game again. I have to do a lot of things around the house myself, but I'm good at hanging in there and I'm one of the fastest packers around."

The family, and Bobbie especially, has made a number of sacrifices to accommodate Jim's whims. They sold their $125,000 home in Englewood and moved into a smaller model. There's no longer extra money around for frivolous things, and Jim has cashed in his children's college saving accounts.

"We now live in a $75,000 house and there's still food in the refrigerator. It's not like we went into the poor house or anything," said Bouton, who is confident he can earn a high income for his family, if need be, by returning to television.

Jim's single-mindedness also caused the Boutons to decide against the large family they had planned. After two children, Jim had a vasectomy and they adopted David be-

134

cause of his concern about overpopulation. "With so many kids in the world whom nobody is taking care of, we don't think any couple has the right to have all the children they can have," explained Bouton.

While in television, Jim took a leave of absence to become a Democratic delegate for George McGovern in 1972. He also kept his children in the Englewood public school system (which is 60 percent black) while their affluent friends enrolled their kids in private institutions.

"Jim is a strong-willed person. He believes in himself and has a vision of how things should be. This makes him an attractive person to me," said Bobbie.

But it's not always the most comfortable way to have a marriage and raise a family. Almost any other woman would have left Jim Bouton during his midlife crisis.

"I understand Jim's need to be alone to sort things out. But where he goes, I go. I'll even follow him to Nome, Alaska," said Bobbie.

Mrs. Bouton is fortunate that Nome doesn't field a baseball team or Jim might have been throwing his knuckler north of the Arctic Circle. The equivalent of this God-forsaken spot in the Bouton saga was Durango, Mexico.

"We had no car and few of the normal appliances. We had to wash our clothes in the sink with a scrubbing board," said Bobbie.

Nonetheless, the ever-positive woman has little negative to say about this experience. "It was good for the kids to live in a different culture. It makes them appreciate what we have now."

While residing in Mexico may have had some good effects, the night Laurie became sick and Jim was away with the team on the road was enough to make them want to return immediately to the United States.

"Laurie had a high fever and we couldn't speak enough Spanish to get a doctor. We had no telephone and no friends. Fortunately, they were shooting the American movie "Who'll Stop the Rain?" nearby and we went down to the site and were able to get someone to radio for help," recalled Bobbie.

Married since 1963, the Boutons have seen all sides of baseball.

"It's really strange being in the minors again," said Bobbie. "The wives are talking about the same problems I used to have, like money and the insecurity of baseball. But their children are just cutting their baby teeth while mine are getting their wisdom teeth."

But one problem she shares with them is loneliness. Bobbie Bouton does not want to be alone. That's why she packs the moment school ends and hauls the family to whatever corner of the continent Jim is lobbing his knuckleball.

"I'm lonely when Jim is on the road. I have three children, so it's not quite so bad. But who likes to be alone at night? And it's worrisome when he's away. You know that there are all these women in all the cities, waiting around the ball parks when the players come out and leaving messages at hotels. You have to push it to the back of your mind," explained Bobbie.

From reading *Ball Four*, Mrs. Bouton is well aware that players aren't prone always to spurn temptations. Former Yankee Joe Pepitone reacted to Jim's words on this subject by saying, "Bouton ought to know. He's one of the horniest bleeps in baseball."

Jim worried about his wife's reaction to the above statement, but all Bobbie said was, "I agree with Pepitone. You are kinda horny."

It seems as though the Boutons never directly addressed Jim's off-the-field activities.

"Bobbie has never looked me square in the eye and demanded to know if I was one of the guys who was playing around," Bouton told *Penthouse*. "And I never said, 'Yes I did' or 'No never.' We talked enough about it, but never really talked about it. I guess if you want to analyze it, it's a matter of respect. I guess neither of us felt we owned the other that much."

Bobbie's good nature carried her over these rough spots with her husband. She told *Penthouse*:

"Laughing and joking about it was the best way for me.

A lot of times I was kidding and I wasn't. That was a tremendous effort. I would say, the night he got home from a road trip and we were in bed, 'I know you have to act horny, but it's okay; you're a good actor.

" 'How long has it been, really?' I would say. I would kid him around that way, but I wasn't completely kidding. Deep down, I guess I wasn't that concerned. But I would hear the other wives talking about what some guy was doing, and I would know his wife would be the 'last to know,' as they say.

"No, I never asked point-blank—except kidding—and I don't think I ever will. If he were playing around he'd lie, right? But, really, I suppose if I saw a picture of him in a nightclub with another woman, I'd want an explanation."

Generally, Bobbie has faith that she can outlast any diversions which might sidetrack her husband.

"The way I look at the situation now is that if some young girl prefers the company of a 39-year-old man with three kids instead of all the other 22-year-old bachelors on the team, she doesn't have enough sense for me to get concerned about it."

During his stay in Savannah, there were no other women in Jim's life. There were just his dreams and his confusion. In Savannah, the family was together and happy.

When there is friction in any family, it is not easy to disguise, and either the partners or the children will give it away. Yet, in a visit to the Boutons at their Savannah Beach house, there was no evidence of any friction. The children were happy and eager. They are proud of their dad and like to share the spotlight. Bobbie smiles and willingly gives interviews about life with her husband. Jim likes the family to be at the ball park when he pitches, and after the game the children and mother wait around the clubhouse door for the father to emerge.

Bobbie Bouton often relates the good years in their marriage to how Jim was pitching, and the best year for them was when Jim won 21 games for the Yankees in 1963. The worst was when he was 4–15 in 1965. The year in Savannah was a good one.

But there is something wrong, for Bouton in more than

a few interviews has stated that one reason for his baseball comeback was a need to get away from his family. He told close friends that he needed to be alone, and among a baseball team, on the mound, a man can be very much alone. In a *Sports Illustrated* interview, Bouton recognized the problems his comeback caused his wife:

"All right, I will admit that the person who suffers in all of this is Bobbie. For whatever benefit this may be for the kids, she's the one left alone to take care of them. But I feel a need to be away from my family for a while right now. I need to be by myself at this point in my life. Look, I'm in my midlife crisis. This is all part of that. It's more than just wanting to pitch. It's wanting to prepare myself for the rest of my life."

And so Bobbie Bouton has to endure, has to "hang in there," a phrase she often uses. She has been with him through the minors, to the heights of New York sports stardom, back down again to his depths as a sore-armed pitcher, ridden to the top once more as he wrote a best seller and became a famous TV personality, and then seen him chuck it all to become a minor leaguer once more.

"I married a jock. He's going to die a jock and I don't mind at all," Bobbie told *Penthouse*.

She has dealt with baseball and TV groupies, and she has come through a strong, resilient person. And at this stage one would think the marriage could endure anything after all they have been through and the apparent love one sees when the family is together.

But something is wrong. Jim Bouton has mentioned some domestic problems to a few people, including his Savannah roommates and manager. But for now these problems were put aside as the family made plans to go to Atlanta.

Part Four
Atlanta

17

The Return

As Jim spent his first hours in Atlanta, he just couldn't stop smiling.

Bouton was very pleased with himself. At age 39, he had done the impossible. He had made it all the way back after taking an eight-year sabbatical. And he did it the hard way, throwing his knuckler in almost every hellhole minor league baseball has to offer. For a 39-year-old man simply to survive the two summers in the bushes was an accomplishment. To prevail and win out at the end—that was a miracle. No one, not Sandy Koufax, Bob Feller, Cy Young, or any of the greats could claim this feat. He alone understood the magnitude of his accomplishment.

"I beat all the odds. When I sit back and think of all the things I had to overcome to get here, I find it hard to believe that I made it. There were just so many obstacles," explained Bouton.

Once again, there was little time for reflection. He had one day to become reacquainted with a major league setting and then the first-place Los Angeles Dodgers would be waiting for him. So Bouton donned the Atlanta uniform and headed out to the stadium for pregame practice. The size of the park simply overwhelmed him.

Atlanta Stadium is one of the new antiseptic facilities. From the outside it looks like something out of a science fiction movie. Inside, there's a huge electronic scoreboard which directs the cheers, there are brightly colored plastic seats, and everything is lit by fluorescent lights, giving the place the appearance of a large, sterile dentist's office. Overall, it leaves the impression of being modern, plastic, and simply too new.

Although Jim had appeared in every major league stadium during his first time around, he had become accustomed to the intimate minor league fields. Now he was like a rookie catching his first-ever look at the big leagues. There were few words and a good deal of pent-up emotions evident.

"Two years ago I would dream of this moment, putting on a major league uniform again, and in my daydreams I would see myself crying," Bouton told the press. "But when the moment came, it was different. I have earned this uniform and I belong here. I didn't have to cry."

There were no tears for Bouton, just joy and that special feeling that one receives by reaching a goal. But now he had to prove himself all over again. The questions about his intentions and sincerity lingered in the minds of his teammates, opponents, the media, and fans. Bouton didn't think about having to please anyone. He had struggled and won. He had made it back when the world was ready to bury him, and Jim just assumed that everyone would understand what his feat entailed and would respect him for it.

His reception in the Atlanta locker room was much warmer than the one he had received in Savannah. Don't get the impression that the Braves were overly thrilled to have a 39-year-old pitcher, who might one day do a book on them, in their midst. Still, the open hostility and hateful looks which made him feel more out of place than a Jew at a KKK meeting were absent.

"These guys know what I've been through. A lot of them played in Savannah and they realize how hard it is to win twelve games there. In fact, some of them never won twelve games in any minor league season. So they know I've done well," said Bouton.

A number of the players recalled Jim's serious, hard-working approach in spring training. They also were aware that the Braves had the worst pitching in the National League (if not all of baseball) and if this strange Bouton guy could get people out, they were ready to welcome him with a smile and a warm handshake.

Most of the Braves reacted like Jerry Royster. "When Bouton came, there were all these media people around and the big hype was something," said Royster. "Everybody was asking all the players what we thought of Bouton. How could we answer that? None of us really knew him. When he was winning those World Series games, most of us were in Little League," added Royster, who is 25.

In fact, the articulate infielder bought a copy of *Ball Four* just to see what all the fuss was about. "I thought the book was good, but I could see why some guys would worry about playing with Bouton. Actually, I think most of our players really didn't care that much one way or another about him," noted Royster.

Jeff Burroughs, the Braves' top hitter in 1978 and an All-Star, offered this observation: "Bouton's got to be somewhat crazy to be doing this. But most of us are a bit crazy. If he produces, then nobody will care what he did or didn't do in the past."

The key was being successful. Jim simply had to do well and there was going to be little time. Baseball had no use for a middle-aged celebrity, even if he threw a knuckleball. The elders of the sport, many of whom came under attack in *Ball*

Four, remembered the book vividly and would have liked nothing better than to see its author humiliated.

Bouton tried not to ponder all of this. In fact, he hadn't even thought much about the Los Angeles Dodgers. "If I started worrying about the Dodgers now, I'll go crazy by the day of the game. I just want to enjoy things now," Bouton told his friends.

Jim spent the day before his second major league debut running in the outfield, playing pepper, shagging fly balls, and doing all the things ball players engage in to make it look as though they are not just standing around with nothing to do. Once again, Bouton was striving to be "one of the boys." Above all else, he didn't want to stick out. If people refused to accept him, he'd at least try not to be noticed.

On this weekend, when the Braves were floundering in last place about 25 games out of the top spot, Jim Bouton was the star. The Atlanta front office was deluged with media requests for tickets from all over the country. When Bouton took the mound the following afternoon, *Time, Newsweek, Sports Illustrated, The Philadelphia Bulletin, Detroit Free Press,* and many others would be there to record the event. But all this was still one day away. Now Bouton had a chance to observe his new teammates in action.

The night before Bouton made his comeback, the Braves behind another 39-year-old knuckleballer, Phil Niekro, knocked off the Dodgers.

"We have an understanding of the knuckleball here in Atlanta," said Braves owner Ted Turner. "Phil Niekro shows what a man can do with it, so we know what to expect from Bouton."

Throughout his trek through the minors, Jim always asked that his knuckleball not be compared with the elusive floater thrown by Niekro. "Stacking my knuckleball against Niekro's is like comparing everybody's fast ball to Tom Seaver's. It's not fair," said Bouton.

Niekro had won 22 percent of Atlanta's games during the last five summers and was a nineteen-game winner on a last place club in 1978.

144

"If Phil were with a really good team, he'd win 25 to 30 games every year," observed Bouton, who was hoping that the Atlanta fans would be satisfied with another knuckle-baller who might win just half as many as Niekro.

Bouton saw Niekro take care of Los Angeles and felt better about his prospects. Maybe the Dodgers just have a tough time with the knuckleball, he thought.

Jim also noticed some differences between his old Savannah teammates and the Atlanta players. "In the Southern League, the dugouts were smaller and people seemed more enthusiastic and into the game. Of course, being in a pennant race had something to do with that. In Atlanta, most guys sat far apart and seemed very low keyed."

At that time, the Braves were just another downtrodden team playing out the waning, meaningless games of the season, longing to go home and forget about all that happened during the summer. But when Jim Bouton took the mound the next afternoon against the Dodgers, it could hardly be classified as just another ball game.

18

Time Warp

Sunday, September 10, 1978, was a perfect day for baseball. The sun was bright, the temperature in the middle 70's, and there was little wind.

These were also lousy conditions for a knuckleball. This mysterious pitch works best when the wind is swirling like a small twister or blowing briskly in the pitcher's face. A good deal of humidity and a dose of thick, heavy night air also helps. All of this acts as a catalyst, making the pitch schizophrenic and difficult to hit far distances.

But none of these elements was present. It was just a nice afternoon in Atlanta, a good day for a picnic.

This day should also go down in baseball history—everyone agreed about that. But no one was really sure how to classify it. Questions lingered. Just who is Jim Bouton and why was everybody so excited about him? He'll never make the Hall of Fame. He had only two fine seasons and the last of those occurred fourteen years ago. His lifetime record was 62–61.

If anything, his activities off the field made Jim Bouton a star. There was *Ball Four*, television news, later a situation comedy, and a few bit parts in movies. The book was big news in 1970, controversial stuff. But a reading of it in 1978 shows that it was fairly mild. All it said was that ball players drink, take pills, and mess around like most of the American male population. Perhaps the hottest item in the book was that Bouton revealed that Mickey Mantle once hit a home run when he had a hangover.

"Today Mickey Mantle is on a beer commercial saying if he had the right beer, he would be in the beer drinker's Hall of Fame," Bouton explained, then added that he expected no lingering animosity over *Ball Four*.

So this was the return of a celebrity to the game, perhaps in the same vein as former Dodgers' first baseman turned actor Chuck Connors making a comeback.

Yet, those who had talked with Bouton and had seen the man struggle and sweat during his minor league odyssey knew it was more. It was the final chapter of a real-life fairy tale, a story for those with romance in their hearts. He was "Rocky" in the flesh, receiving his shot at the big time. Like the movie character portrayed by Sylvester Stallone, Bouton had paid his dues.

Finally, it was decided that this day was just something special, something that couldn't be defined. One writer suggested that it was the start of a second lifetime for Bouton. Jim now holds the record for the most lifetimes in the majors.

So Jim Bouton was going to begin his second baseball career against the Los Angeles Dodgers, the top club in the National League. The mood in the stands was festive. A crowd of 11,108 (4,000 less than had been predicted, but twice the usual Atlanta late-season Sunday crowd) had shown up, attracted by Bouton's return and a postgame Big Time Wrestling Match. By putting wrestling on the bill, the Braves did little to dispel the notion that this was just another Ted

Turner gimmick, like the time the Atlanta owner decided that he'd give Manager Dave Bristol "a vacation" and run the team himself from the bench.

When Bouton emerged from the dugout and sprinted to the mound, the fans stood and cheered. Those in baseball uniforms and behind typewriters were the skeptics; these folks in the stands were the romantics. They wanted Bouton to succeed because if he did, it might mean that there was hope for them, too.

Many of the fans had followed Jim's progress in Savannah through the Atlanta papers. Here was a man who had gone out, dirtied his hands, and been laughed at. No one wants to grow old, be told that he can't do this or that. Bouton refused to acknowledge all of these societal stigmas and the fans loved him for it.

Now as he stood on the Atlanta mound and watched the 11,108 people standing and cheering, he knew that it was all worth it. This one moment was the ultimate gratification. Everything seemed surreal. It had been eight long years since he had gripped a ball in the majors. Now here he was at 39, the crowd on their feet and applauding, and Los Angeles's Davey Lopes at the plate.

"I was in territory no one has ever been in before," said Bouton.

Jim stepped forward like a courageous pioneer, flipped his knuckleball, and hoped. It floated down the middle as the Dodger hitter watched and umpire Eric Gregg raised his arm indicating strike one.

Bouton was relieved.

"I had this fear that I might go out there and not throw a strike. I was just hoping to get that first one over," recalled Bouton.

Lopes watched four more of his offerings, and on the fifth pitch of Jim Bouton's second major league lifetime, Davey Lopes struck out. The crowd roared and Bouton emitted a sigh of relief.

The next Dodgers batter was Bill Russell and he tapped a roller to Braves third baseman Bob Horner. Two out.

148

After Russell was Reggie Smith, one of the awesome swingers in baseball. A perennial All-Star, he was good for 30 homers a season. Bouton lofted his knuckler to the plate and Smith hit a miserable roller to Horner. Three outs and the inning was over.

Bouton dashed from the mound. The crowd again was on its feet. Jim Bouton had put the side out in order and it was easy, as easy as it had been against the Orlando Twins and the Columbus Astros. But these weren't a bunch of naive kids playing in the bushes. No, the guys Bouton retired were the Dodgers, for God's sake. They were in a World Series. They were the biggest boys in baseball's big show and all they could manage was a strikeout and two lousy ground balls.

Jim was convinced that he had been vindicated. As he approached the dugout steps at the end of the dramatic first inning, he thrust his hands over his head like a victorious prizefighter. The crowd roared louder.

For the 40 or so friends and relatives who had come to Atlanta to watch Bouton, it was a time warp. On his back was number 56, the old Yankee numeral and one of the last links to the glory days. He still had the special windup which caused his hat to fall off. And more important, he was getting big league hitters out, like in the old times. It was enough to make one believe in dreams, miracles, and Santa Claus.

The second inning was more of the same. Steve Garvey, Ron Cey, and Dusty Baker all went down before Bouton's soft knuckler. Once again there was a standing ovation and Bouton again raised his hands over his head while heading into the dugout.

"I had raised my hands over my head only once before," recalled Bouton. "Dick Radatz, who was Boston's top reliever in the 1960's, used to do that after he came in and mowed people down. So one time I threw a two-hitter in Boston and stood on the dugout steps and did that. The Boston fans were furious because I had stolen Radatz's victory sign and I got hate mail for weeks. I decided not to do that any more in Atlanta after the second inning because I didn't want it to become a trademark or anything," added Bouton.

Suddenly, the third inning was over and Jim had yet to allow a hit. A walk was the only blemish. The fans gave him yet another standing ovation, this one longer and louder than the first two. People in the press box said things like, "Wouldn't it be something if the S.O.B. threw a no-hitter?" and "Do you believe what that old man is doing to the Dodgers?"

The fans just glanced at each other and smiled. This was even better than "Rocky." This time, the underdog wasn't going to just go the distance, he was destined to come out a winner. Patroling the aisle was a big yellow duck supplied by a local radio station. "Quicksy Quacker Is a Bouton Backer" said the sign he carried.

After three innings, Bouton's "severe case of butterflies disappeared." He was in just another ball game like those in Savannah, Portland, Mexico, and the New Jersey sandlots.

In the grandstands, Michael Bouton was being an objective observer. "I'm not going to say anything until Dad makes it through the fifth inning."

Michael wasn't given an opportunity to express his opinions. In the fourth inning, the dream of a no-hitter, and a brilliant debut, ended. Like Bouton's fast ball, it vanished without warning.

Bill Russell led off with a walk. Then the count went to three and one on Reggie Smith. Smith took the next pitch and umpire Gregg called, "Strike two." Smith argued for five minutes and was tossed out. Dodger manager Tom Lasorda emerged from the dugout and discussed the call for another five minutes.

Meanwhile, Bouton stood idly on the mound.

"This is bad," Bobbie Bouton said of the break in the action. "A knuckleball needs so much concentration."

"They were just trying to intimidate me," said Bouton. "They wanted to get the upper hand."

Whether the break in the action caused Jim's downfall no one really knows. One thing was certain: when play resumed, he couldn't throw his knuckleball over the plate.

Billy North, who replaced the exiled Smith, then walked.

Garvey, Baker, and Cey ripped singles, then Bouton fell behind on Rick Monday. Jim threw the Dodger outfielder a mediocre slider and saw the ball disappear over the 402-foot sign in center field. Before you could say comeback, Los Angeles had five runs.

This time when Bouton departed from the mound, there was no standing ovation. Rather, the crowd was quiet, almost shocked. It was apparent that Bouton's dreams weren't the only ones which had been shattered.

Bouton lasted another inning and allowed a solo homer to Davey Lopes. He left the game after five innings for a pinch hitter. He allowed six hits, walked four, and was hung with six earned runs as Atlanta was enroute to an 11–5 thrashing.

During the sixth inning, an announcement came over the public address system: "Jim Bouton will now hold a press conference."

Afterwards, Bouton would be blasted for being self-centered and an egomaniac because he called a meeting while his teammates were still on the field.

"I never called my press conference," Bouton explained later. "I was sitting by my locker when the clubhouse man came over and asked if I would mind meeting with the press right away because they were waiting outside the locker room. Since he asked, I thought it might have been okay, so I agreed. You have to realize that I had just been hit hard and there were still a lot of people around who wanted me to disappear. I guess this was a ploy to make me look bad."

Whatever the circumstances, Bouton met with the press in the middle of the game. His mood was pleasant and he tried very hard, though not always succeeding, to leave the impression that he was pleased with what had just transpired.

"I think I proved I belonged out there. I showed that I had good enough stuff to make major league hitters swing and miss and I was able to get them out. I'm satisfied even though I didn't get them out consistently," said Bouton.

Noticing the skeptical expression of his audience, Bouton added, "If Elvis Presley were to come back from the dead, some sportswriter would say, 'Not bad for a start, Elvis, but is all this a publicity stunt?' Then another writer would ask, 'Okay, Elvis, you're back, but what if your first record isn't a hit?'

"I don't know if this is the beginning or the end for me. I just know I had fun out there today. I went on the field before the game thinking how lucky I was."

While the crowd seemed to appreciate the significance of Bouton's debut, Jim could see that this wasn't true of the media. He felt a need to defend himself.

Jim presented his case in another fashion. "When Sir Edmund Hillary climbed Mt. Everest, no one asked him if he was going to build a country club on the peak. They just admired him for getting there and that's how it should be with me."

He then called up his old refrain. "I deserved this chance as much as anyone. I won twelve games in Class AA. I had twelve complete games. A lot of guys in the majors now never accomplished that much.

"Look, I'm not a gimmick. It's taken me two years to get here and I didn't embarrass myself. I proved that I belong," said Bouton.

Jim Bouton may have thought he was back in the family of major league baseball, but the sport was hardly ready to accept its prodigal son. This he soon discovered.

Bouton as Bozo the Clown

If Jim Bouton were a Broadway play, he would have closed after opening night. His reviews were terrible.

"Bouton should never have been out there," said Davey Lopes of the Dodgers. "It was a disgrace to baseball. It was all a gimmick, a publicity stunt. He made a farce out of the game. It's quite obvious what he's done."

"His knuckler is like a blooper," said L.A.'s Ron Cey. "It's like almost every pitch was a blooper."

Rick Monday, who homered off Bouton, said, "It's not for me to judge what kind of pitcher Bouton is. If they put Bozo the Clown out there, my job is to hit him. I don't know, maybe Bozo would have had better stuff."

There were also complaints about Bouton's style.

"He ran off the field throwing his hands up in the air like Rocky," said Lopes. "I don't think the Braves' players cared for that, but none of them would say anything because of Ted Turner."

"The whole thing was a joke," said Reggie Smith. "Eventually, Ted Turner is going to have to stop making fun of the game."

"I thought Bouton was supposed to be a knuckleball pitcher. He threw me only two or three knucklers and the rest were sliders and change-ups," noted Monday.

And on it went. Cincinnati Manager Sparky Anderson said that Baseball Commissioner Bowie Kuhn should look into the matter since Bouton was pitching against contending teams and could alter the pennant race.

Jim Bouton had definitely made a splash, just as he had thought, but the reaction certainly wasn't what he had expected.

"I'll admit that I'm slow," said Bouton. "But that shouldn't matter as long as I'm successful. In Savannah, I'd tell people that I was throwing my knuckler 80 to 90 percent of the time when I was using it only about 60 percent. I also used to say that my knuckleball was thrown harder than Niekro's when I knew that it really wasn't. All of this was part of the salesmanship job I had to do. Let's face it, nobody was going to be interested in a 39-year-old junkball pitcher with a slow knuckler. They would hardly look at me as a strict knuckleball pitcher," explained Bouton.

Jim's fastest pitch made it up to the plate at 70 miles per hour. His knuckler drifted in at 60 mph. The average fast ball thrown in the majors is about 85 mph, so it was easy to see the difference in Bouton's offerings.

Criticism of Bouton continued to mount. His teammates weren't fond of his early press conference or the manner in which his gestures played to the crowd. They considered him a prima donna placed in their midst by Turner. More important, they thought he did not deserve the chance he was receiving.

All of this unnerved Bouton. When Braves Manager Bobby Cox said, "I don't know if he'll start again," Bouton worried even more. What had happened to the four or five starts the Braves had promised him?

His next emotion was anger. He felt betrayed by the media which had treated him so kindly during his stay in the minors.

"I just can't believe this. They expected me to go out there, after eight years away from the majors, and beat the Los Angeles Dodgers. It just should've been enough that I made it all the way back and got some people out during my first try. It's not fair," said Bouton.

There were more items in Bouton's self-defense.

"I don't mean this as a knock, but the guys who relieved me were even worse. They allowed ten hits and five runs in just four innings. That just goes to show that the Dodgers can hit anybody."

The debate raged on. But the fact remained that Bouton was superb for three innings and, as one writer pointed out, "When was the last time any Braves pitcher worked three straight hitless innings? . . . Bouton deserved a chance, especially with a team like Atlanta which has started some of the worst pitchers in the history of the sport."

For every "Bouton backer," there were dozens like *Atlanta Journal* and *Sporting News* columnist Furman Bisher, who wrote the knuckleballer off in an article titled "The Grand Delusion." The piece was scathing, suggesting that Bouton had returned to sell more copies of *Ball Four* or gather material for a *Ball Five*.

Always sensitive to his image in the press, Bouton was appalled by his detractors. The only thing he really had risked in his comeback was humiliation. The wealth and fame would be there once again if he returned to television and writing. But if he went back now, with his ego feeling as though the Dodger sluggers had just knocked it around in batting practice, he would be a defeated man.

Bouton just had to go out there again. He couldn't let it all end like this. Two years on buses, chasing around the country just to have the ride halted by one lousy inning. Jim kept telling himself that he was the "Bulldog." He could use his stomach to will his way through this crisis, too. But Bouton was scared. He dared not consider the consequences of another shelling.

Meanwhile, Ted Turner and Bill Lucas had no choice but to give Jim another opportunity. They, too, had looked like fools when Bouton was bombed. It was decided that he'd pitch four days later against the San Francisco Giants.

20

"Cool of the Evening"

Jim Bouton often talked about experiencing the "cool of the evening." That's the time of night after a pitcher has performed admirably. He'd done his job and now didn't have to worry for the next three days until his next start. There was time to sit back, reflect on and enjoy what had just happened.

Conversely, when a starter feels as though he just stepped out of a war zone because of all the bullet-like line drives zipping past his head, the time between his starts is anxiety ridden. He thinks about things, just as a successful hurler does, but instead of savoring the past there is just a nagging worry that the disaster might happen again.

There was little company for Bouton in his misery. Bouton's family returned to New Jersey after his Atlanta debut. He had no roommate, since, "I would drive whoever got stuck staying with me crazy. The phones would always be ringing from reporters and old friends."

Also, no one wanted to be closely associated with Jim after his initial shelling. Bouton was a controversial figure and not very successful at the moment. Being thought of as a friend of Jim's was not the ideal tag to have after one's name—especially when the Braves' manager and front office (except for Turner) and the baseball establishment didn't consider Bouton one of their favorite people.

There is also something in the nature of professional athletes which prohibits players from becoming too close. Having a good friend only causes pain when one of the parties is traded or released. Since the sport is a highly competitive business where the supply of players greatly exceeds the need, it's easy to understand why looking out for Number 1 is the real name of the game. In baseball, everyone is an acquaintance but there are few friendships in the manner of Jim Bouton and his old roommate Roger Alexander.

So Jim bided most of his time alone. He was a newcomer to the squad and that added to his isolation. Some players, like pitcher Micky Mahler, did take the knuckleballer to dinner and try to make him comfortable, but most simply ignored him. None of the Braves would openly criticize Bouton, not when Atlanta owner and their boss, Ted Turner, remained a supporter of the former Savannah Brave. In the ever-changing world of professional baseball where a man is viewed according to how he did in his last game, Jim Bouton's stock was suffering a recession.

No one was more aware of this than Jim. But he thought back to the past, to the times when there were just the heat and discomfort of the night instead of the "cool of the evening." He had survived and would do so again.

"I pitch best when I'm scared," said Bouton. "I was terrified pitching in the World Series and I was great."

There's no doubt that Bouton was effective in baseball's autumn classic. His 2–1 record and 1.50 ERA attest to that claim.

When he took the mound against the San Francisco Giants just four days after his difficult debut against the

Dodgers, it was the same as a World Series game to Bouton. The same fear was present. Another display of mediocrity could manifest itself in his baseball funeral.

"I felt that I had to do well to take the pressure off. Ted Turner and Bill Lucas were getting the heat from the press and I had to do it for them. They gave me my chance," recalled Bouton.

It was another clear day; this time the game was being played in San Francisco's Candlestick Park, where there is always a nice breeze. It was good knuckleball weather. Inside, Bouton felt the pressure and he was afraid. But this time he didn't experience the sharp, colliding emotions which had accompanied his return four days before. This was just another important game, like the one he had worked in the Southern League playoffs against Orlando.

Once again, Bouton started well, holding the second-place Giants scoreless in the first two innings. San Francisco broke through for a run in the third when Jim fielded a bunt and threw wildly to third base, attempting to force a runner.

Then he began to concentrate, paying intense attention to every movement he made. He took care to make sure that every knuckleball was released with the proper push-off. He called upon the confidence which had vaulted him past the Braves in Richmond and over Nashville in his Savannah opener.

This time, Bouton didn't lose control of his knuckleball in the crucial situations. Now he made the pitches to the spots which left the hitters spitting, swearing, swinging, and missing. After six innings, he had allowed only three hits, two of them being looping, opposite field doubles. The Giants went down like the Montgomery Rebels and the Jacksonville Suns.

"I just used the same stuff against San Francisco that worked all summer in Savannah," said Bouton.

The score was knotted at 1–1 in the top of the seventh when Atlanta Manager Bobby Cox sent in a pinch hitter for Bouton. In that inning, Atlanta scored three times en route to a 4–1 win. Hard-throwing sidearm reliever Gene Garber, whose offerings must have seemed like a Concorde jet compared to Bouton's gliding knuckler and palmballs, saved Jim's first win since July 11, 1970.

It had been eight years, two months, and four days since Bouton's last major league victory. So much had happened in the interim and all he could think about now was what his critics and those guys who had knocked him around in the amateur leagues were saying now.

After the contest, he was gracious. "I'm thrilled, but it's just enough to be back in the majors. Winning on top of it all is miraculous and it's always nice to silence your critics."

In professional athletics, production is the only factor in discussing a man's worth. A player could be a sexual and social deviant, but if he excels and can stay out of jail, he's worth a ball park full of guys who have saintly characters but can't hit a curve ball. By winning, Bouton had gained the grudging respect of his teammates. In the same way Jim had changed the views of his comrades in Richmond and Savannah, by performing what seemed to be unimaginable, he forced the Braves to reconsider their first opinion of him.

However, his opponents were far from impressed. "It's a disgrace for Bouton to be in baseball," said San Francisco's Bill Madlock, a lifetime .300 hitter who was blanked by the knuckleballer. "His ball doesn't do anything. The only thing I can say is that he beat us."

"My little boy is two and he throws better than that," said the Giants Mike Ivie, who was also hitless against Bouton. "Everything he threw was soft."

"I must be doing something right," countered Bouton. "I've pitched eleven innings and eight have been scoreless. Those are major league hitters trying to get hits off me. Either I'm pretty good or they're pretty lousy."

The victory made Jim Bouton a legitimate big leaguer. It guaranteed nothing more than another start four days later in the Astrodome against Houston, but it took the pressure off. And this time, it wasn't the knuckleballer who was humiliated, and that was perhaps the most important thing to Jim. Finally, he could begin to enjoy being a major leaguer once again. Up to now the worries and sheer emotions of the comeback had preoccupied him.

"You know it's just nice to be back in the Big Show. Aside from the obvious differences, like the ball parks and larger crowds, it's good being back because the meal money is higher ($21, to $7.50 in the Southern League) and I don't always have to look for cheap places to eat," said Bouton.

In the major leagues a ball player has several people at his disposal with an Avis "We Try Harder" attitude. His spikes are polished daily by the clubhouse man, there are always a nice variety of sandwiches available before the contest and small buffets of chicken and roast beef for postgame meals. Beer is served on tap along with a wide variety of soft drinks. In Savannah, a soggy sandwich or hot dog from the concession stand was all a bush leaguer could expect. Beer was drunk from the can.

As for atmosphere, the majors try to make their dressing rooms almost like offices. There are carpeted floors, bright fluorescent lights, and piped-in music. The manager has a large, executive-like office and the trainer has his own quarters. In Savannah, Bobby Dews had an office about the size of an outhouse. Actually, the place seemed more like a walk-in closet, about nine feet deep and four feet wide.

The players' locker stalls are twice as large in Atlanta as those in Savannah. Of course, the Atlanta clubhouse was air-conditioned and heated, so it was sure to have the ideal temperature at all times. One trip through the Southern League is enough to convince a player that these cities must not have discovered air conditioning yet.

Jim Bouton liked the conveniences and pampered lifestyle of a big leaguer. He was nurtured on it with the New York Yankees, and having one more taste of it at 39 was a special treat. He was a middle-aged man allowed to have another Christmas with Santa Claus paying him one more visit.

After the San Francisco game, Jim also was able to experience "the cool of the evening." It was just like the old days in New York when he would win regularly and then couldn't wait to get back out there again, convinced that success was imminent.

When he stepped out into the Astrodome, he had that confidence which marked his great years with New York. In the last three months he had pitched only two bad games. He was getting people out, and he was doing it time and time again.

The Astrodome is a special place to Bouton. It was with Houston that he finished his first major league career in 1970. Also, the Astros are prominently featured in *Ball Four*. This fact inspired one fan to bring a sign to the game proclaiming, "Bring back Norm Miller." Miller was Bouton's roommate with Houston and a featured character in the book.

Compared to his first two opponents, the Astros' lineup could very well have been one from the Southern League: it featured a bunch of nonentities named Puhl, Gonzalez, Cruz, Bochy, and Walling. But it wasn't going to be as easy as it appeared.

J. R. Richard was the Houston pitcher. If you ever saw J. R., you'd never forget him. At 6-foot-8 and 237 pounds, he tends to make a strong physical impression. In his huge hand, the baseball seems like a golf ball. When J. R. flung his frame toward the plate, the baseball looked more like a kernel of corn. His pitches had the speed of a stock car—fast, faster, and fastest.

"Richard is so big and takes such a long stride toward the batter that I swear you can smell his breath after he lets go of the ball," said Philadelphia's Rich Hebner.

So this Paul Bunyon character, a man who should be single-handedly chopping down the redwood forests or playing center for the New York Knicks, was Jim's latest in what seemed like a long course full of obstacles.

The game meant a great deal to Richard. He was aiming for a 20-game winning season and he needed eleven strikeouts more to get a major league mark in the area for right-handed pitchers.

For those who enjoy seeing brains pitted against brawn,

this was the ideal matchup. J. R.'s pitches usually jetted up to the plate at 95 mph, while Bouton lobbed his collection of soft stuff in the 60-70 range. It was like racing a Volkswagen against a Ferrari.

Richard was determined to throw as hard and as long as he could. It was his goal that no Atlanta batter would hit a fair ball off him.

For 6¹/₃ innings, he almost succeeded. He held the Braves hitless and fanned eleven to break Tom Seaver's right-handed pitcher season strikeout record of 289.

Meanwhile, Bouton was plagued with control problems early in the game and permitted a run each in the third and fourth innings. But the knuckleball slipped into gear and Jim retired twelve of the last thirteen men he faced.

After seven innings, the score was knotted at 2–2 and Bouton left for a pinch hitter. J. R. also departed, suffering with a stiff elbow. The Ferrari and the Volkswagen had finished in a dead heat.

There were few disparaging remarks coming from Bouton's opponents.

"He definitely was not impressive, but he got the job done," said Houston Manager Bill Virdon.

"A lot of people laughed at Bouton because he doesn't throw hard, but what difference does it make?" asked Houston third baseman Enos Cabell. "Some pitchers blaze it in and still can't get anyone out. If he refines his knuckler so it moves even more, maybe he'll stay around until he's 50. Why not? It seems like other knuckleball pitchers do."

The second straight impressive outing had Bouton ecstatic. It also enabled him to reply to his critics. "All this business about my getting everyone out because they're not used to my slow speed is ridiculous. In batting practice coaches lob the ball in and they hit it in the seats. Speed has nothing to do with why they're not hitting me. Rather, it's the movement. My balls move once, usually down and very sharply right before they reach the plate."

The veteran then attacked the scouting system of major league teams. "I'll tell you why you don't see many junkball pitchers around like Eddie Lopat or Stu Miller, anymore. It's because of the large Central Scouting Bureau. Today scouts are only looking for a 6-foot-2 kid from someplace like California who can just throw hard. They never bother to get to know the kid and see if he has guts or if he's smart. They just look for size and speed. They'd never sign a lefty like Whitey Ford these days. He wouldn't fit their mold just like a young Jim Bouton wouldn't. And that's too bad for baseball because they're missing out on a lot of talented pitchers who aren't big and don't throw really hard. They just get people out."

At this point, Bouton was on the complete offensive, ready to overwhelm his critics like the Nazis blitzing Poland. "I understand why guys get upset when they can't hit me. Sports is a big macho field. It's okay to overpower someone, but it's not all right to outsmart them, which is what I'm doing.

"There's also more than just a little jealousy involved. The Dodgers complained about the circus-like atmosphere because of all the media. What's a World Series if not a circus atmosphere. They were just upset because the cameras were pointed away from them for once."

If there were any notions that Bouton had mellowed or was willing to take the punches like a boxer with his hands tied behind his back, these remarks ended that speculation.

The few Bouton supporters in the sport and the media immediately recognized the source of the criticism. "It all goes back to *Ball Four*," said Bobby Dews. "People who don't really know him think he's some kind of traitor. I've never seen anyone attacked en masse like they've done to Jim. It's like there's some kind of conspiracy against him and the book is to blame."

Bouton agreed. "I was hoping that the resentment over *Ball Four* would be over by now. Well, when most players hear the name Bouton, they say that I'm the guy who wrote those bad things about baseball. In people's minds, I fall under the category of 'wise guy' and 'controversial.'"

Jim was very aware of what Thomas Wolfe experienced when he wrote *Look Homeward Angel*. This was a thinly veiled fictionalized account of the people in Wolfe's hometown of Asheville, North Carolina. When Wolfe returned home as a triumphant author, he was treated like the carrier of some contagious disease. This gave him material for a sequel which became *You Can't Go Home Again*, in which Wolfe told how all his old friends now hated him.

Well, Bouton "went home again." He knew that the reception would be cool, but he didn't expect such verbal abuse.

"For two years I honored and played their game. I bowed before them by going through the minors, riding the buses and working my way up. I earned my chance and deserve some respect, and all I get is criticism and am treated as if I'm some guy who walked straight out of a TV studio and onto a major league mound. I even get people out and they refuse to be contrite."

The criticism deeply wounded Bouton. He had always prided himself on the excellent press he had received throughout his career. Even in the minors, the reporters were generally kind, receptive and respectful. Suddenly, he reached his goal and it seemed as though every one had turned on him. When a man is alone, having temporarily severed ties with his family, it's difficult to handle such a negative reaction. There was no one to share the burden, and it weighed heavily on Bouton.

"Frankly, the criticism has drained me. There's pressure everywhere and I've been on the spot all season. I couldn't afford the luxury of having two bad games in a row because everyone was looking for an excuse to get rid of me. Mentally, it's been a rough year," explained Bouton.

Exhausted or not, the year wasn't over for the former author. His next start was against the powerful Cincinnati Reds. The Reds weren't winning with their usual regularity, but they still boasted of an awesome lineup, including Pete Rose, George Foster, and Johnny Bench.

This time, there were ideal conditions in Atlanta for a knuckleballer. The air was heavy and a light rain fell during most of the game. The wind was brisk and unpredictable.

In a word, Jim was superb. The Reds' Ken Griffy led off the contest by swinging so hard at a knuckleball that he wound himself like a corkscrew and then fell down as the umpire called strike three.

For eight innings Bouton teased Cincinnati. Employing his arsenal of knuckleballs, palmballs, and change-ups, like a snake charmer uses a flute, he had the Reds under complete control. After eight innings he had allowed only five hits and a pair of runs. The problem was that the Braves managed only a single run and Jim suffered a 2–1 loss. That lowered his major league record to 1–2 with a 3.40 ERA and his lifetime big league mark slipped to 63–63.

But that hardly discouraged Jim. Once again, he was a success. Pete Rose failed to hit safely in three tries, and earlier in the season he had gone 44 consecutive games without being blanked. Only the muscular George Foster was able to handle the 39-year-old pitcher as he lined a pair of solid singles.

Cincinnati Manager Sparky Anderson, who just three weeks before had called Bouton a disgrace and asked the baseball commissioner to rule him out of the big leagues, became a Bouton supporter. "Jim Bouton was great. We were lucky to get the runs off him that we did. We just didn't hit the ball hard off him," said Anderson.

Anderson is a neat man with a military mind. His players are not allowed to wear beards, mustaches, or long hair. Anderson likes to talk about the virtues of the United States and loyalty to the flag. He is the type of baseball man Bouton ridiculed in *Ball Four*.

In Anderson's comments about the former author there was more than a tinge of sarcasm. Nonetheless, it was evident that Anderson was trying to come down on Bouton's side in case the knuckleballer became a big success. After his earlier remarks, Sparky was simply paying homage when he had been proven wrong.

"The Braves are lucky," said Anderson. "They've come up with a third starter to go with Phil Niekro and Larry McWilliams. I have no doubt that Bouton will be in the starting rotation next year."

While not all that Anderson said could be recorded as gospel, he was the first member of baseball's upper echelon to publicly praise Bouton.

Meanwhile, Bouton was adopting a cynical tone with reporters. His charm, wit, and patience remained, but it was clear that he was growing weary of all the criticism.

"So how were my reviews?" he asked the reporters.

"I never knew how well I pitched until after the game," said Bouton. "It doesn't seem to matter if I got people out, I had to look good, too. I'm revolutionizing the game. Now there'll be no more need to try a young pitcher against batters. All you'll need to do is bring the rookie out and let him throw on the sidelines while his opponents watch. If the opponents think he looks good, he's a success. If not, send him back to the minors."

These certainly weren't the words of the polite Jim Bouton who just six months before was begging to pitch for anyone, anywhere.

Interestingly, word of Jim's success against Cincinnati even reached the White House. President Jimmy Carter had invited Pete Rose to Washington in honor of his 44-game hitting streak, second only to Joe DiMaggio's all-time 56-game record.

Carter asked Rose, "How are you hitting?"

"I'm only hitting .298 and I'm doing kinda bad right now," said Rose. "In fact, I couldn't even hit old Jim Bouton and he throws like this," added Rose, making a slow arching motion with his arm.

"He throws like me, a softball pitcher," said Carter.

So Bouton's feat of stopping Rose had reached the center of the government, but it did little to ease his mind.

Bouton was tired and he confided this to friends. "There's been so much pressure every time I've pitched. I just have to keep performing well and can't afford much of a slip-up. I'm making my last start of the year against the Reds again and there's a possibility that I could get hit hard.

"If the Reds hit me, everybody will just say that Bouton can't get them out the second time he faces a team. It used to be that I couldn't get people out the second and third time I faced them in a game, but I disproved that. It just seems that people keep putting more and more obstacles in my way."

In Bouton's encore against the Reds, he was clubbed, shelled, and stomped. Three innings, seven runs, and home runs by Pete Rose and George Foster clearly ended Jim's season on a down note.

"My control was awful and I just didn't have it," said Bouton. "It happens to every pitcher at some point."

The former TV star seemed happy that the year was over. His face displayed more lines than usual and he began to look like a man nearing 40.

"I always look older when I'm tired," said Bouton. "I guess I've been worrying and I haven't gotten the sunshine like I did in Savannah. A tan keeps me looking better. But this has been a long year and it's taken a lot out of me. It's been a tremendous season but it was filled with pressure and there never seemed to be a time when I could relax. Every game was crucial. It'll be nice just to sit back and not worry for a while," concluded Bouton.

Part Five
Epilogue

21

Looking Back

It was one of Jim Bouton's final days with the Savannah Braves. He and roommate Stu Livingstone sat in the corner of the Grayson Stadium clubhouse. As always, Livingstone had a chaw of tobacco in his mouth about the size of a tennis ball.

"Damn, I'll be glad when this whole thing is over," said Livingstone, who then spat a stream of juice into the empty plastic cup in his hand.

"Nah," said Bouton. "You love it and you know it."

"No, I'm telling you that I've had enough. We've been going at it every day since March and I'm tired," said Livingstone.

"You're only saying that because you got shelled last night. If you had struck out the side, you'd want the year to go on forever," said Bouton.

"Maybe, but I doubt it."

"Well, I don't want it to end. You really don't appreciate how good this is until it's over," said Bouton.

"Bull," said Livingstone with another squirt into the cup.

"Seriously, I'm projecting myself into December. There's snow on the ground outside and I'm sitting at a table with a big dinner in front of me and having a glass of wine. Now, I'm thinking how good it was to be able to sit in the Savannah Braves clubhouse, listen to the radio, and talk baseball," said Bouton, speaking more to himself than to anyone else while staring out dreamily at the other players.

"I want to memorize every detail about this place. When December comes I want to be able to sit back and feel everything the way it feels now. I want to remember all that being back in baseball meant to me," said Bouton.

"Yeah, maybe," mumbled Livingstone.

"You know, this isn't a bad way to spend part of your life, just sitting here in the clubhouse listening to the radio," concluded Bouton.

There was quite a bit for Bouton to memorize about 1978. The record book will show that his major league return was nothing special. He had a 1–3 record and a 4.97 ERA, which placed him right in the middle of the putrid Atlanta pitching staff.

But how can one put a numerical value on a natural wonder or a miracle? In the baseball world, that's exactly what Jim Bouton is. His arm had died in 1964 and his then sagging career was finally buried in 1970. Yet, he had the audacity to launch a comeback seven years later when most ball players would have retired and the rest of society is comtemplating making out a will.

Numbers really mean very little to Jim. For example, he doesn't worry about age. In fact, he jokes about growing old, as he told *Sports Illustrated:*

"They say I'm old now. That's funny because when I'm really old, I'm going to have a lot of fun. I'm going to have some stories to tell. All the kids on the block are going to want to listen to strange old Jim as he sits in his rocking chair and talks about the old days . . . All this stuff is just getting me ready to be an old man. I'm going to be a great old man." One doubts that an aging Jim Bouton will have time to sit around and recount tales of the good old days. He'll probably be leading a movement for elderly rights. Jim is just not one to sit back for anything, because there's something burning inside him, continually driving him to cross a new frontier.

What makes Bouton different from the others who must tackle ridiculous challenges is that he doesn't believe he is able to do the impossible. No, contrary to popular belief, Jim Bouton doesn't think he can move mountains. But he is quite sure that he can remove more than enough rocks to make an impact. That was the key to his success in 1977–78. He just kept tossing aside the seemingly endless number of boulders which were placed in his path.

"Sometimes I ask myself if I would have gone through with it if I had known all the obstacles that would be in my way. I'm not positive, but I think I would have," said Bouton.

To Jim Bouton, the struggle was worth it. It was worth the mental and physical strain, worth the $250,000 loss of income, worth the problems it created with his family. Just being able to sit in the Grayson Stadium clubhouse and discuss baseball with Stu Livingstone made it all worthwhile.

Of course, there was more to the quest than just playing ball again. As Bouton said, "If I just wanted to play, I'd have stayed around my house and played semipro ball."

Rather, it was the pursuit of something that had never been done before. It wasn't an impossible dream because the timeless and unpredictable knuckleball has unlimited potential. But his vision was improbable to say the least, and by far the stiffest challenge he had ever faced.

Only a man with a large ego would have set out on such a venture, and Jim certainly does not have a shortage in the confidence department. If he did, he never could have made his way up the minor league ladder by "willing" things to happen or retire batters by pitching with his "stomach." This ego also made him well aware that he had pulled off something special and he was upset when others didn't see it that way.

"I did something remarkable, and I did it in the public eye in a business where you can't hide. A father can hide his son in a bank or vice-president's office. A man can carry a friend or relative in a newspaper office or in almost any office because the public never knows. In baseball, they know.

"I thought I would have made the cover of *Time* and *Newsweek*. Bruce Springsteen made the cover and what does he do besides play a little music?"

On several occasions Bouton has compared himself to deceased superstars, saying he was like one of them returning to life.

"I plead guilty to having an overstated sense of my own self's worth. But what I've done is something that I or anybody else should be proud of," said Bouton.

The comeback reaffirmed Jim Bouton's belief in himself. He often talks about his instincts, "the voices in the back of my head that tell me to do things." If there is anyone that he listens to, it's those voices. The voices told him to leave television and its rooms without windows. The voices ordered him back to the diamond, to be a child again. And like a good son, Bouton heard the voices, followed their instructions, and discovered that the voices (whoever they may be) knew best.

But the voices didn't have all the answers. Jim said that he was "in a midlife crisis, preparing myself for the rest of my life." Well, when the 1978 season was drawing to a close, he said, "I guess I'm now in the middle of my midlife crisis." The future is still uncertain, like the plot of a mystery with several possibilities but no apparent solution.

After the season ended, Bouton and his wife were unable to solve the difficulties between them and they separated. His two sons moved in with him while daughter Laurie stayed with her mother.

Over the winter fire, Jim mulled over his options. There

was always television work or there was trying to become an established major league hurler at 40.

Another possibility he pondered was writing a book, a subject he is very defensive about and seems to have postponed until his playing days are over.

"Some people still think I'm a farce and that I'm doing all this just to write a book. That's like saying Tom Seaver pitches so he can do yogurt commercials.

"And what if I did write a book? Would it diminish what I have accomplished? Can anybody name one athlete who ever came back after so long a time?" asked Bouton.

One man who wants Bouton to author another book (aside from Jim's agent and publisher) is Bobby Dews. "I really do hope that Jim does a book. What he accomplished was truly amazing and it's a great story that should be told. I'm not afraid of what he might write. When Jim left the team, he gave me an autographed copy of *Ball Four* and I read it over the winter and didn't find anything that upsetting in it," said Dews.

Bouton still has these feelings that he should be doing more than just playing ball, writing books, or reading scores in front of a camera. He has a genuine concern for the plight of the poor and strong political convictions about how to make the world a better place. There were many times when he acted on this sense of public service by attending benefits, visiting hospitals, and the like. One example occurred in Savannah, where he showed up at a Muscular Dystrophy Rally as an uninvited guest and helped them raise money.

Jim has been called self-centered, and it's true that he is a person with a large ego. But he is also a man who cares about doing what he considers "the right thing." For this reason, he signs countless autographs, shows more than the usual patience and kindness to fans and writers, and is active in charitable affairs.

When the former Savannah Braves Manager Bobby Dews

thinks back on 1978 and Jim Bouton, one conversation with the former author remains in his mind.

"It was late in the season and Jim came up to me and asked what I thought of his chances of getting called up. I told Jim that he had about as much of a chance of making it as I did and I didn't think I was going anywhere.

"So the season ended and Bouton got called up to Atlanta. I figured I was wrong. Then I got a call from the Atlanta front office asking me to be a coach with the big league club. So I was right. Both of us somehow managed to make it. It's incredible when you think about it," said Bobby Dews.

After 1978, no one can call Dews a "busher" anymore. Nor can anyone label Jim Bouton a "gimmick." Rather, they fall under the heading of success.

By the end of the season, Jim Bouton had turned the heads of many who despised him and had become an inspiration to countless fans across the country. Wherever he played, Jim's mailbox was full of letters from elderly people saying things like, "They made me retire when I was 65 and I could still do the job. Don't let them ever tell you that you're too old. Go out there and show them what older people can do if given a chance." During some of his more depressing times, Bouton would read over these letters and feel revived. One of the more cherished items he received from a fan was a poster of a little knight with a small sword challenging a huge dragon. The inscription under the knight read, "You've got to believe."

There were thousands of fans who had faith in Jim Bouton and followed his progress. In Savannah, when he began winning and receiving a good deal of national attention, the local press and the ball club handled numerous calls each week checking on the status of the knuckleballer. The idealistic and romantic sides of Jim's comeback had captured the imagination of many sports fans who were appalled by the seemingly greedy, gruff athletes who had removed much of the fun and joy from the game by their petty, businesslike personalities.

The baseball establishment generally found the new

Bouton an engaging and refreshing person. Instead of wanting to negotiate his contract, all he longed for was a chance to play ball. It took them time to realize this, and there are still several holdouts who view Bouton only as "the traitor who wrote that awful book."

But the list of Bouton converts is impressive. There was Baseball Commissioner Bowie Kuhn, who refused to act on Cincinnati Manager Sparky Anderson's request that Jim be banned from the game because he "was a farce." Kuhn, who had said that Bouton "did the game a grave disservice" when *Ball Four* was released in 1970, supported the knuckleballer this time, ruling that he had proved himself in the minors. Then Bouton performed admirably against the Reds and Anderson found himself chanting his praises, too.

Atlanta General Manager Bill Lucas, who considered Jim too old and not a serious prospect at the start of 1978, also came to Jim's side. "Never have I seen anyone give up as much for the game as Jim Bouton," said Lucas. "I admit that I wasn't for Jim at first, but he proved me wrong. Now I'm a Bouton fan. I want him to do well. We need pitchers desperately on the Braves, and if Jim can do the job, that's one less pitcher I have to find."

The fans and the brass weren't the only ones responding to Bouton's quest. His Savannah roommates improved, matured, and learned from being around him.

Roger Alexander weathered a severe slump, the kind that usually would have confined him to another mediocre year; he righted himself and revived his floundering career during his stay with the former author.

Stu Livingstone pitched the best baseball of his life, posting a 1.32 ERA while rooming with Bouton. Both seemed to have learned the value of internal fortitude from Jim.

Finally, there were the dozens of major leaguers who were quick to criticize Bouton after his initial big league performance was less than a success and later had to retract their statements when Bouton prevailed. These turnabouts pleased Jim as much as anything else he accomplished. It made his return an even more satisfying experience.

"This was the greatest summer of my life," said Bouton.

177

"After it was over, I just felt so good about the experience and myself. There are so many things I'll never forget. I beat all the odds and that's obviously something to be proud of."

No one has ever topped Bouton's act. Once again, he had been "Warmup Bouton" in the world of the "naturals" and the skinny kid with the big heart had won out. To Jim Bouton, that was the most important thing.

Statistics

JIM BOUTON'S CAREER RECORD

YEAR	CLUB	W–L	G	GS	CG	IP	H	R	ER	BB	SO	ERA
1959	Auburn	1–4	7	4	1	33	28	28	21	23	28	5.73
	Kearney	2–4	15	5	2	55	55	40	33	29	56	5.40
1960	Greensboro	14–8	28	24	12	194	175	79	59	51	121	2.73
1961	Amarillo	13–7	28	27	13	197	179	80	65	81	151	2.97
1962	New York	7–7	36	16	3	163	124	63	59	59	71	3.99
1963	New York	21–7	40	30	12	249	191	79	70	87	148	2.53
1964	New York	18–13	38	37	11	271	227	100	91	60	125	3.02
1965	New York	4–15	30	25	2	151	158	89	81	60	97	4.83
1966	New York	3–8	24	19	3	120	117	49	36	38	65	2.70
1967	New York	1–0	17	1	0	44	47	31	23	18	31	4.70
	Syracuse	2–8	16	15	4	91	98	38	34	19	29	3.36
1968	New York	1–1	12	3	1	44	49	20	18	9	24	3.68
	Seattle	4–7	27	8	0	99	93	48	44	35	53	4.00
1969	Seattle	2–1	57	1	0	92	77	48	40	38	68	3.91
	Houston	0–2	16	1	1	31	32	16	14	12	32	4.06
	Houston	4–6	29	6	1	73	84	53	44	33	49	5.42
1970						Did Not Play						
1971–74						Did Not Play						
1975	Portland	4–1	5	5	4	41	32	13	10	16	17	2.20
1976						Did Not Play						
1977	Knoxville	0–6	10	8	2	53	61	35	31	14	19	5.26
	Portland	5–1	9	9	5	58	52	33	29	26	14	4.50
	Durango	1–4	6	5	0	29	33	19	16	13	16	4.97
1978	Savannah	12–9	21	21	12	159	114	68	48	63	76	2.77
	Atlanta	1–3	5	5	0	29	25	18	16	21	10	4.97

WORLD SERIES RECORD

YEAR	VS	W–L	G	GS	CG	IP	H	R	ER	BB	SO	ERA
1963	Los Angeles	0–1	1	1	0	7	4	1	1	5	4	1.29
1964	St. Louis	2–0	2	2	1	17	15	4	3	5	7	1.56